The FBI
v.
The First Amendment
By Richard Criley

How the FBI attempted to "neutralize" the National Committee Against Repressive Legislation (NCARL)—founded in 1960 as the National Committee to Abolish the House Committee on Un-American Activities (HUAC)

Published by the First Amendment Foundation

Richard Criley

Richard Criley was one of the founders of the National Committee to Abolish HUAC (today NCARL), and staffed its midwest office, the Chicago Committee to Defend the Bill of Rights, from 1960 to 1977. He is currently a member of NCARL's National Coordinating Committee.

Criley was born in Paris, France in 1911, the son of an American artist. On his mother's side, he was descended from William Whipple, a signer of the Declaration of Independence, and on his father's side from Giles Corey, who was pressed to death in the Salem Witch Trials of 1692.

He grew up near Carmel, California, attended Stanford University and the University of California at Bekeley, where he graduated with honors and did two years of graduate studies in history. He served three years as a civil affairs staff officer of the U.S. Army in Europe during World War II.

In 1985, Criley received the Earl Warren Civil Liberties Award of the American Civil Liberties Union Foundation of Northern California.

The First Amendment Foundation gratefully acknowledges the support of the C.S. Fund (469 Bohemian Highway, Freestone, California) for this and other cutting edge educational projects we are undertaking.

Library of Congress Catalog number: 90-83117
ISBN 0-9627705-0-7

Book design and production courtesy Synthesis Concepts Inc., Chicago, IL.
Calligraphy by Peter Fraterdeus.

Table of Contents

Preface

Speeches sometimes make history. In our own day, the Address that has made the most profound impact is Winston Churchill's "Iron Curtain" speech at Fulton, Missouri in 1946. It is not too great an exaggeration to say that it set the course of our foreign policy—and not our foreign policy alone—for the next generation. More than this it set the tone, as it were, for public opinion about domestic as well as foreign policy for the next half century.

War psychology, war economy, and war diplomacy permeated the Cold War—a misnomer, for the whole period was dominated by actual war and preparation for war. The popular acceptance of these policies, in turn, introduced a new era in American morals and character.

We now take for granted a "national enemy." It is so loosely used and so taken for granted that few of us realize that in the past the United States had been almost alone among nations in not having a "public enemy." Since World War II we have busied ourselves with hostilities in distant Vietnam, in Korea, Nicaragua, Cuba, Iran ... and above all with the Soviet Union. The military dominates not only our national budget, but our diplomacy, our international economic policies, our science, our industry, and *above all our thought.* It dominates public discussion, elections, strategy, the whole of our global affairs.

Until a decade ago, Congress listened to a reading of Washington's Farewell Address every year.

They might do well to revive that inspiring habit, which would remind them again (in Washington's words):

"Nothing is more essential than that permanent, inveterate, antipathies against particular nations be excluded, and that in place of them, just and amicable feelings toward all should be cultivated. The nation which indulges toward another habitual hatred (or habitual fondness) is in some degree a slave. It is a slave to its animosity or to its affection ..."

Through forty years of military hostilities, we have been a slave to our fears and prejudices. This is the underlying current in the investigations conducted by the FBI, described in this pamphlet—including the recent ill-conceived investigation of The Committee in Solidarity with the People of El Salvador (CISPES).

A further development in the post-war years is that which this study addresses with authority: It is the growth of secrecy in American public life. Secrecy is, and has always been, the most effective tool of authoritarian regimes. Americans have heretofore looked upon it as alien to a democratic society or government. Now we have developed secrecy to the point where we have our own Official Secrecy Law*, and our vastly inflated national organizations, the FBI and CIA, whose policies are enshrouded in secrecy. This pamphlet provides elaborate evidence of how one of these organizations—the FBI—has attempted to conceal from the American people what their government is about. As in past centuries, secrecy, once given official blessing, knows no limits. We are witnessing, even now, the preposterous lengths to which it can be carried.

The Congressional hearings of 1988 should make clear to the whole American people that

* The Supreme Court denied Samuel Morison's petition for certiorari, leaving Mr. Morison the first person to be convicted under the "espionage" and "theft" statutes for giving classified information to the press. The Fourth Circuit had rejected Mr. Morison's challenge that theft of government property and espionage laws do not apply to disclosures of information to the press; the Supreme Court refused to review this decision. U.S. v. Morison, No. 88-169 (October 17,1988).

there are no effective safeguards against the abuse of secrecy—a conclusion which the recent trial of Lt. Colonel North now re-enforces.

A nation which embarks upon policies of secrecy in military and international affairs will find it easy to enlarge the concept of "defense" to encompass domestic affairs as well. Let us conclude with that admonition from the greatest of our champions of liberty, Thomas Jefferson:

"If there be any among us who would wish to dissolve this Union or to change its republican form, let them stand undisturbed as monuments of the safety with which error of opinion may be tolerated where reason is left free to combat it."*

Jefferson's First Inaugural Address as quoted from Commager, Living Ideas in America, p. 147-148

Henry Steele Commager
1989

ACLU Foundation of Southern California co-counsel Paul Hoffman and Douglas Mirrell in *Wilkinson vs. FBI*, review blanked out documents submitted by the FBI in response to pre-trial discovery motions under the FOIA, August 1983. The total surveillance and disruption file of the FBI in the case: 132,000 pages.

Foreword

My office is filled with a dozen large boxes of FBI documents totalling more than 60,000 pages. They are a portion of the FBI's own record of its attempt to destroy a small civil liberties organization in which I was a participant. Despite the FBI's extensive deletions, it is still possible to reconstruct the story of a massive, extended campaign to prevent a group of citizens from exercising its First Amendment freedoms of speech, press and assembly and to petition the government for a redress of grievances.

This intervention of the FBI into my life and the lives of my colleagues was but a tiny segment of a vast operation code-named COINTELPRO, which the Senate Select Committee on Government Operations, after a far-reaching investigation, described as follows:

COINTELPRO is the FBI acronym for a series of covert programs directed against domestic groups ... Many of the techniques used would be intolerable in a democratic society even if all of the targets had been involved in violent activity, but COINTELPRO went far beyond that ... [T]he Bureau conducted a sophisticated vigilante operation aimed squarely at preventing the exercise of First Amendment rights of speech and association, on the theory that preventing the growth of dangerous groups and the propagation of dangerous ideas would protect the national security and deter violence.

—Final Report, Book III, Staff Report, April 23, 1976.

It is hard to visualize the total impact of COIN-TELPRO and related FBI operations on the pattern of life in our country, and its chilling effect on the exercise of our freedoms. The case history presented here may help to bring it into focus. The fact that the author and his co-workers were the targets of the FBI's covert war provides the added dimension of personal insight.

Although most of the events described here occurred before or during the 1960s, they are relevant today. The threat of recurring FBI abuses is real, and indeed may be imminent. The "state of mind" of the FBI, revealed in its effort to block publication of this story of FBI invasions of the First Amendment, and in fact to delay it for many months, suggests something less than a resolve to reform its ways. (See appendix.)

Paul Conrad cartoon, Copyright 1975, Los Angeles Times.
Reprinted with permission.

The "Thought Police" are still with us

After the 1976 public exposures of the FBI's flagrant abuses of constitutional rights, changes were made. Congress broadened the purview of the Freedom of Information Act to include CIA and FBI documents. Guidelines drafted by Edward H. Levi, Attorney General in the Ford Administration, imposed restrictions on FBI investigations in First Amendment areas. William Webster, a federal judge, was appointed FBI Director with a mandate to carefully supervise FBI operations.

Early in the Reagan Administration, however, the President signalled a change in policy. He pardoned the only FBI officials ever tried and convicted of violations of constitutional rights.* In 1981, he issued Executive Order 12333, authorizing the CIA and FBI to engage in secret political spying to combat foreign "terrorism" on U.S. soil. In 1982, EO 12356 gave almost unlimited discretion to government officials to classify and withhold documents from the public. In 1983 Attorney General William French Smith issued new FBI guidelines, rescinding many of the restrictions imposed by Levi.

Under the Smith guidelines, full investigations, using informers and other intrusive methods to collect information, could be undertaken without requiring a preliminary inquiry to establish reasonable cause to believe a crime was occurring. Sensitive operations could be launched without written authorization from headquarters. "Foreign

*FBI officials W. Mark Felt and Edward Miller, who had authorized illegal break-ins in the investigation of the Weather Underground, were indicted in 1978 and convicted. President Reagan issued the pardons without examining the trial records.[1]

Counter Intelligence/International Terrorism" guidelines which remain classified, were more permissive than those governing "Domestic Security" areas.

The CISPES Investigation

Only recently has the public learned how these administrative changes affected FBI policies and practices. In the past year, a partial release of documents through the Freedom of Information Act revealed that the FBI was again seriously abusing its investigative powers. The publication on July 14, 1989, of the report of a 17-month inquiry undertaken by the Senate Intelligence Committee, confirms the earlier charges of flagrant irregularities. From 1981 to 1985, the FBI conducted two investigations which ultimately involved 1,330 groups and 2,370 individuals who opposed Administration policies in Central America. The FBI so far has released only 1200 heavily censored pages of the 3600 in the Headquarters file. This much is known:

In 1981, the FBI began an investigation of the Committee In Solidarity with the People of El Salvador (CISPES) on the basis of an unexplained request from the Reagan Justice Department alleging violations of the Foreign Agents Registration Act. The FARA investigation was closed after three months, for lack of evidence. But curiously, two months before any investigation was authorized, FBI Headquarters sanctioned the infiltration of the Dallas chapter of CISPES by contract employee Frank Varelli, in clear violation of the Attorney General's Guidelines.

In 1983, a new investigation was initiated under the secret and permissive guidelines for "Foreign Counter Intelligence/International Terrorism." On the theory that other groups opposing U.S. Latin-

* The old "front groups" rationale was dredged up to enable the investigation to expand beyond CISPES chapters and affiliates to any of the hundred organizations whose work brought them in touch with CISPES or its members. [Statement of Dr. Ann Mari Buitrago, FOIA Inc. January 27,1988]

**Sanford J. Ungar, dean of the School of Communications at American University, who has made an in-depth study of the FBI, wrote in a recent article: "powerful institutional forces and biases skew the Bureau's view of the United States and the world. And while it is shrinking, there is still an Old Guard that has enormous influence over FBI policies and practices." New York Times Magazine, May 15, 1988. For a further example of the survival of the J. Edgar Hoover state of mind, see Nightwatch Special Report, Vol 3, No. 8, "The FBI, Perennial Target of the Left," by W. Raymond Wannal. Wannal was a Special Agent from 1942-76, and was one of the senior agents directing the COIN-TELPRO operation against NCARL. Security and Intelligence Foundation, 2800 Shirlington Rd., Suite 405, Arlington VA, 22206.

American policy might be "CISPES fronts," the FBI extended surveillance into ever widening areas, ultimately involving 52 of the 59 FBI Field Offices.* When the cover of FBI contract employee, Frank Varelli, was blown, the Justice Department's Office of Intelligence Policy and Review looked into the case and found that the FBI's stated justification failed to satisfy the Attorney General's Guidelines. The investigation was officially closed in June, 1985. No direct financial connection between CISPES and insurgent Salvadoran guerrillas was ever substantiated. The two year investigation had involved at least 20,000 FBI employee hours, and repeated violations of First Amendment protected activities at public demonstrations, and religious gatherings. Yet, according to the FBI's official explanations, all of the basic decisions were made by the lowest level of Supervisory Special Agent at FBI Headquarters, in crass violation of procedures instituted by then-Director William Webster to supposedly protect the public's constitutional rights.

In his testimony before the Senate Intelligence Committee, Oliver Revell, Executive Assistant Director of the FBI, declared that then-Director Webster, had never been informed of the CISPES investigation. Revell, the highest official to admit involvement, justified the five years of political surveillance as necessary to national security despite the lack of evidence of criminal wrong-doing. Senate panel member Senator Arlen Specter told Revell that instead of facts, "You have only a state of mind of FBI investigators."**[2]

The Bureau's CISPES file demonstrates the lusty survival of past attitudes and practices which dealt with the investigative subjects as mortal enemies to be destroyed. A memo from the New Orleans Field Office, dated 11/1/83, declared:

It is imperative at this time to formulate some plans of attack against CISPES and specifically against individuals who defiantly display their contempt for the U.S. Government by making speeches and propagandizing their cause...[3]

Information derived from members of such right wing groups as the Young America's Foundation (YAF), the Unification Church ("Moonies"), and the John Birch Society was paid for by the FBI and disseminated to Field Offices. Some of the material appears to have been gathered by break-ins and other illegal means.[4]

The FBI used methods including undercover infiltrators, mail covers and wiretaps to obtain political intelligence and names of activists in the CISPES related surveillance of political and campus organizations.*[5]

A cloak of secrecy still surrounds the operations of the FBI. Under guise of protecting "national security" and FBI "sources and methods" and utilizing the latitude of censorship granted by Executive Order 12356, only a small fragment of the CISPES investigation has been made public.** The continuing concealment of the record diminishes the credibility of current FBI Director William Sessions' claim that the investigation "was not a return to the days of COINTELPRO."[6] The conclusion of the report of the Senate Intelligence Committee has an ominous ring:

> The CISPES case was a serious failure in FBI management, resulting in the investigation of domestic political activities that should not have come under government scrutiny. It raised serious issues that go to the heart of this country's commitment to the protection of constitutional rights. Unjustified investigations of political expression and dissent can have a debilitating effect upon our political system. When people see that this can

*A Boston Globe editorial 1/27/88 summarized: "Americans freely expressing their opinions were placed under surreptitious surveillance. They were photographed covertly. Reports about their lives were entered into the FBI's computer files and circulated to other government agencies, because they spoke at legal meetings, attended legal demonstrations, published legal newspapers and made legal petitions to their government for redress of grievances."

**Not only are current FBI documents withheld, but documents relating events of 20 and 30 years ago are still zealously guarded. Censorship to protect the identities of long deceased informants still applies. Compare Wilkinson et al v. FBI.

happen, they become wary of associating with groups that disagree with the government and more wary of what they say or write. The impact is to undermine the effectiveness of popular self-government.

The FBI "Library Awareness" Program

The degree to which the Cold War still dominates the thinking of the FBI to the exclusion of First Amendment concerns is illustrated by yet another current operation, the "Library Awareness Program." For more than ten years FBI special agents have been visiting libraries across the country to recruit library employees as volunteer informants to report on foreign students and other foreigners using library research facilities. Librarians have protested this violation of long standing library policies of confidentiality, but the program has been defended by FBI Director William S. Sessions before the Senate Judiciary Committee. The Bureau's rationale for the program, an official 32-page report entitled, "The KGB and the Library Target," concludes: "The FBI must logically pursue any contact between a Soviet national and an American citizen, regardless of where the contact occurs or the profession of the person contacted..." [7]

Racism Persists In The FBI

An FBI campaign in the fall of 1984 is indicative of the FBI's persistent institutional racism. Since post-Civil War Reconstruction, Black people in southwest Alabama, where they constitute a majority, had been deprived of all meaningful participation in the electoral process. Change came with the Voting Rights Act of 1965, when a massive voter registration drive was launched. Even then, in cases where Black registered voters outnumbered whites, the old power structure still dominated the elections through fraudulent use of absentee ballots and other corrupt election practices.

Ultimately, in the late 70s, civil rights leaders succeeded in collecting legitimate absentee ballots from the numerous elderly shut-ins and workers with distant jobs. By 1982, Blacks had won majorities on county commissions and school boards in five southwestern counties. In 1983, they won a seat in the State Senate and three in the Assembly.

In the fall of 1984, approximately 50 FBI agents descended on southwest Alabama, visiting the homes of more than 1,000, mostly elderly, Black voters. Aided by the State Police (long notorious for its internal segregation), the FBI rounded up a bus-load of elderly Blacks, and overnight took them 165 miles to Mobile, Ala. for questioning. Rumors flew that scores of Black leaders faced criminal charges for voter fraud.

Eventually, eight Black activists were indicted. All won acquittals or reversals except for two who plead guilty to minor misdemeanors to avoid lengthy trials. This attempt to restore power to the white minority power structure through intimidating poor and elderly Blacks failed, thanks to a vigorous counter campaign waged by the civil rights movement.[8]

As further evidence of internal racism, law suits filed in 1988 by a Black agent and by a group of Hispanic agents charged discrimination. The Black agent, Donald Rochon, when assigned to the Omaha Field Office, was subjected to a campaign of harassment by white agents. This included the defacement of a photo of his son with an ape's picture, telephone threats to sexually assault his wife, and death threats against himself. When he filed an official complaint, FBI officials, instead of investigating his grievances, transferred him to Chicago, along with the two ring-leaders of the campaign against him. One of these promptly organized a group of white Chicago agents to take "retribution against Rochon" for his complaints.[9]

In late September, 1988, U.S. District Judge Lucius Bunton in El Paso, Texas, ruled that 311 Latino agents who sued the FBI had "demonstrated a pattern and practice of discrimination related to conditions of employment and promotions." Bernardo Perez, the number 2 man in the El Paso Field Office, had filed the suit in January, 1987, and subsequently was joined by two-thirds of all the Hispanic agents employed by the FBI.[10]

" . . . you have the right to remain silent . . . "

Paul Conrad cartoon, Copyright 1977, Los Angeles Times.
Reprinted with permission.

The Inheritance From The Past

The FBI's current violations of constitutional rights flow directly from its past.

The spirit of J. Edgar Hoover, the Director who shaped the FBI in his own image, lives on in much of the top officialdom and the senior agents who were recruited, trained, motivated and indoctrinated by him. To understand the FBI of today, we need to know the FBI of yesterday.

G-Man Above The Law

During his lifetime, J. Edgar Hoover succeeded in cultivating the image of the ultimate public servant—incorruptible, dedicated, courageous, and single-minded in the pursuit of malefactors. It was deemed unpatriotic to even question his opinions.

Hoover came to wield power beyond any appointed official in our times. Under his skillful administration, he elevated a minor agency, beset by corruption and ineptitude, into a mighty bureaucracy which he controlled as his personal fief.

Hoover exercised his power to force the political and moral thinking of Americans into conformity with his concepts of good and evil. Inevitably, Hoover collided with the Constitution.

He chose to ignore its limitations. In particular, he never accepted the basic principles of the First Amendment, and waged a holy war against what he considered the heresies of his time. He was un-

Paul Conrad cartoon, Copyright 1975, Los Angeles Times.
Reprinted with permission.

daunted by the fact that the Constitution under which he operated expressly forbad the punishment of dissent.

Thus the FBI came to embody a profound contradiction. While it won public veneration as the very model of scrupulous law enforcement, it was, in fact, a flagrant and chronic violator of the supreme law of the land. The unique talents of Director Hoover allowed these opposites to coexist until his death, when at last the walls began to crumble.

During Hoover's near half century in office, from 1924 to 1972, nine Presidents were elected and selected their key aides to administer the Executive Branch. But none chose to replace the Director of the FBI. No Attorney General, theoretically his superior, could exercise meaningful control or supervision. Some tried.

In 1939, the FBI developed a special classification for persons it deemed "dangerous," who were placed under a listing of "Custodial Detention," for roundup and detention in case of a national emergency. In a memorandum dated July 16, 1943, Attorney General Francis Biddle ordered Director Hoover to cancel the classification and to stamp the following message on each Custodial Detention Card: *"This classification is unreliable. It is hereby cancelled and should not be used as a determination of dangerousness or of any other fact."*

The FBI formally complied. Then, without notifying the Attorney General, the FBI listed the same persons under a new classification, "Security Index"—just as if the Attorney General had never acted.[11]

Nor were Congressional checks and balances of any consequence. Certain House and Senate Committees became the FBI's partners-in-crime, while Hoover kept private files on the personal lives of legislators as a further "insurance policy" against any hostile action or criticism.

Public Relations FBI Style

Nationwide, thousands of FBI special agents tracked local publications and radio broadcasts for any unfavorable stories or criticism of the FBI and its Director. When possible, steps were taken to suppress the unfriendly publicity. If this failed, the Bureau, through the services of its vast network of media friends, could, without attribution, unleash its powerful thunderbolts of counter-propaganda.

The Crime Records Division was in reality a high powered public relations department, headed by one of Hoover's most trusted aides. It employed a host of writers and research specialists to write the Bureau's numerous books, articles and pamphlets (often ghost-written for the Director), and to prepare "blind memos" and other "public source" material which the Bureau covertly distributed to selected media contacts.

The Shadow Of The Cold War

J. Edgar Hoover was never comfortable with the growth and encouragement of radical or even liberal political trends. Prior to World War II, the Depression years and the Roosevelt New Deal allowed the American Left and, within it, the Communist Party, to expand its influence and associations in many areas—the labor and youth movements, and cultural fields, including the Hollywood movie industry. During the War, the political alliances necessary to defeat the Fascist regimes of Germany, Italy and Japan led to further acceptance of left-progressive goals.

However, the Cold War began with astounding

suddenness, even before the last shots of the war had been fired. The dropping of the atomic bombs at Hiroshima and Nagasaki signalled a warning to the Soviet Union and the Third World that the United States possessed the ultimate weapon and would assume the leadership of the "free" world. Our old enemies, Germany and Japan, were now our allies; our former ally, the Soviet Union, was now the ENEMY.

Hoover used his FBI to define and identify appropriate new enemies at home as well. Congress passed the Internal Security Act of 1950, proclaiming that our nation faced the deadly threat of the "world-wide Communist conspiracy." Earlier, the FBI and the Justice Department had implemented this concept in the Smith Act trials which resulted in the jailing of a score of leaders of the Communist Party.

The surge of anti-Communism, orchestrated by the FBI in its covert manipulations of the press, engulfed our world. Since guilt was now primarily ideological, it mattered little whether a person had been an actual member of the Communist Party, or was branded as a "fellow traveler." As the political scene was painted with the broad brush of guilt-by-association, many Americans who had participated in building a CIO union, or some cultural forum were enmeshed in the nets of the subversive hunters. What had been legal and even commendable yesterday, had ex post facto, become some kind of a crime in the brave new world.

The House Un-American Activities Committee—A Useful FBI Tool

The FBI needed a vehicle through which to filter its information and identification of domestic "enemies." To convert confidential material into "public source" information which could be disseminated to the media required a laundering agency. This very special role was played by the House Un-American Activities Committee (HUAC), the Senate Internal Security Subcommitttee (SISS) and the state "little HUACs." These inquisitorial committees, officially independent legislative agencies, were, in fact, largely dependent upon the FBI for their sources of information and general direction. The FBI secretly provided the bread and meat for the Congressional hearings by targeting the persons to be pilloried and making informers available to testify. The committees also gave the FBI a lethal means of *neutralizing* its chosen targets without need to prove any violation of the law. Congressional testimony had the additional advantage of being libel free, depriving the victims of any means to sue for damages, no matter how false and defamatory the testimony, or who quoted the material.

The most active, best staffed and financed of these inquisitorial committees was the House Un-American Activities Committee. After uncertain beginnings as the Fish Committee (1930-32) and the McCormack-Dickstein Committee (1934-35), it hit its full stride under the flamboyant Texan, Martin Dies in 1938. As the U.S. became a participant in World War II, against the Fascist Axis, and as an ally of the Soviet Union, Dies' strident anti-communism and divisive attacks on the Roosevelt Administration were clearly out of step with historical necessity.

In 1946, however, with the changing climate of the emerging Cold War, HUAC became a permanent standing committee, mandated to investigate "subversive and un-American propaganda activities." It was armed with the power to compel testimony under subpoena, and to punish with citations for contempt of Congress.

In the classic confrontational HUAC hearing, witnesses summoned before it were of two kinds, "friendly" and "unfriendly." The "friendlies" were the informers who "named names" in well rehearsed testimony. Most often these were paid FBI infiltrators; others were persons who were supportive of HUAC's aims and purposes, and volunteered their cooperation, as did former Screen Actors' Guild President Ronald Reagan (FBI code number T-10); and some frightened persons who gave reluctant testimony to escape blacklisting. The "unfriendly" witnesses were pilloried in proceedings lacking every element of due process and fairness. They often "took the Fifth Amendment" to avoid being compelled to be witness against themselves and others.

Until the mid-sixties, the news media usually played a negative role, headlining HUAC charges, no matter how outrageous, and giving full and uncritical coverage to the "friendly" witnesses, while downplaying or totally ignoring the testimony of the HUAC victims and critics.

Thousands summoned before the Committee, and more thousands merely named in testimony, suffered ruined reputations, loss of jobs and careers. A few with the temerity to attempt First Amendment challenges to the Committee's right to question ended up serving prison sentences for contempt of Congress. The FBI provided backup services by visiting employers to make sure they were aware of their employees' non-cooperation with the Committee, most often leading to dismissal. The FBI Crime Records Division indexed HUAC hearing records for inclusion in its "public source" information, ensuring that "unfriendly" witnesses would be stigmatized for years to come.

Paul Conrad cartoon, Copyright 1976, Los Angeles Times.
Reprinted with permission.

Internal Security Investigations

Unlike other committees of Congress, HUAC's main aim was not the legislative purpose mandated by the Constitution, but the ideological mission of inculcating anti-Communism and chilling dissent. Its legislative accomplishments, while limited, included sponsorship or support for a series of federal laws which punish ideological speech and advocacy, rather than violent, fraudulent, or corrupt conduct. These laws included the Smith Act, which prohibited advocacy of the violent overthrow of the government, or membership in an organization which so advocated; the Internal Security Act of 1950, which required the registration of "Communist action, Communist front, and Communist infiltrated" organizations; the McCarran-Walter Immigration Act which forbad entry and authorized deportations on ideological grounds; and the Taft-Hartley Act, which required an "I am not a Communist" oath of union officials.

These speech crimes were especially valuable to the FBI because they provided the law enforcement rationale (the FBI calls it the *predicate*) for open ended Internal Security investigations. They were tailor made for the FBI's collection of information relating to First Amendment activities, since political opinions, speeches, political writings and associations were arguably relevant to crimes of advocacy. Paid FBI informers in groups under investigation had lifetime jobs, if their covers were not blown.

Internal Security investigations seldom led to indictments and prosecutions, however. According to the General Accounting Office, which studied a sampling of 676 specific Internal Security cases, there were only four convictions, none of which related to violations of federal law or national security.[12] Countless millions of dollars were spent on Internal Security investigations. As years passed, and the courts blocked prosecution for "political" crimes, they became irrelevant to law enforcement.

Yet, these investigations did serve another purpose, high on Hoover's priority list. They provided the political intelligence needed for the FBI's *neutralization* program. Although they were short on law enforcement, internal security investigations were long on paper work. Files proliferated with geometric progression as new groups and individuals were caught up in the dragnets. Mountains of paper were generated at every level. The investigation of a small civil liberties group, the National Committee Against Repressive Legislation (NCARL), produced over 132,000 pages.

The FBI files were officially inviolable and confidential. The FBI was so certain of the security of its files that few precautions were taken to cover up illicit Bureau operations. Destruction of files like the *DO NOT FILE* file, which recorded FBI burglaries of information (known in the trade as "black bag jobs), was the exception. Special security protected the *JUNE* files, "authorizing" illegal wiretaps. But the COINTELPRO files, which exposed the FBI's intervention into the protected areas of the First Amendment, were kept in Field Offices as well as at the Headquarters. The burglary of COINTELPRO files from the resident agency office in Media, PA, on March 8,1971, opened the first crack in the dike of secrecy and precipitated Congressional hearings. These documents, anonymously mailed to the media and congressional offices, provide a chilling glimpse of the Hoover mind set—his contempt for the Constitution and his abuse of power to disrupt and even destroy the lives of countless individuals whose sole "crime" was political dissent.

Neutralization

COINTELPRO was only the most notorious of the FBI's secret *neutralization* operations. These began in the early days of the Bureau, before the formal creation of COINTELPRO in 1956, and continued after its formal discontinuance in 1971. There were other code names, like the RESPONSIBILITIES program, but most often there was no special designation at all.

Neutralization means *to cause to cease to exist as a political force. Neutralization* was most often not physically violent, but there were notable exceptions. The FBI created situations which led others to commit acts of violence. In Chicago, for example, the FBI sent forged letters to street gang leaders to incite them against the Black Panthers. An FBI informer provided the critical information to a special detail of Chicago policemen assigned to State's Attorney Edward Hanrahan who *neutralized* Black Panther leaders Fred Hampton and Mark Clark with their fatal shotgun blasts. The suicide of actress Jean Seberg was heavily influenced by an FBI "poison pen" letter which falsely alleged she was made pregnant by a Black Panther leader. The FBI used tape recorded conversations from Dr. Martin Luther King Jr.'s bedroom in an apparent desperate attempt to induce his suicide to prevent his receiving the Nobel Peace Prize.

Whether violent or non-violent, *neutralization* was the antithesis of law enforcement. Under the color of law, the Constitutional rights of individuals were violated, systematically and knowingly.

In the dawn of the sixties, the country was beginning to free itself from the suffocating grip of the Cold War. Not surprisingly, one of the first movements to challenge the assumptions of the era chose the most conspicuous symbol of McCarthyism, HUAC, as its target.

THE HANGING TREE

Paul Conrad cartoon, Copyright 1970, Los Angeles Times.
Reprinted with permission.

The NCARL Story

The National Committee To Abolish HUAC Is Born—With A Label

On October 10, 1960, a group of civil liberties activists from across the country met in New York City's Taft Hotel to formally announce the formation of the National Committee to Abolish HUAC. Unbeknownst to the person charged with setting up the initial press conference, the House Un-American Activities Committee had placed the following release in the hands of the wire services and major newspapers at 6:30 P.M. the night before:

The House Committee on Un-American Activities said today six officials of a new national organization trying to abolish the Committee have been identified as members of the Communist party.... target of the House group was the National Committee to Abolish the Un-American Activities Committee... it identified the six officials as...

Dutifully, the *New York Times*, like the rest of the press, picked up the HUAC lead: "Of thirty-four delegates attending, six have been accused by the House Committee of being members of the Communist Party." This theme of the "communist plot" was developed by Fulton Lewis, Jr. in his widely syndicated column a few days later.[13]

These slanted news items did not spring out of

the blue. They were carefully planted by the FBI which had been conducting undercover surveillance of a Los Angeles group, the Committee to Preserve American Freedoms, since its formation in the early 50s, and of its Executive Director, Frank Wilkinson, since the 40s. When the Executive Board of the LACPAF met in June to decide to initiate a national organization to abolish HUAC, word was immediately flashed to FBI Headquarters. Steps were quickly taken to set up a file on the yet to be formed group, alert field offices, monitor the bank account, and record all long distance calls.

By August, the new group was the subject of a Headquarters internal memo, outlining the first active *neutralization* measures to be taken. These were to be implemented by Cartha DeLoach, top FBI official in charge of covert relations with HUAC, the American Legion, and the favored news media contacts. Director Hoover marked his emphatic "YES" over his initial on the memo. Having briefed HUAC Staff Director Francis McNamara, DeLoach provided detailed dossiers on the entire prospective leadership of the new National Committee for a special September 15 edition of FIRING LINE, the official organ of the Legion's National Americanization Committee.[14]

Frank Wilkinson

Frank Wilkinson was the prime mover in the formation of the National Committee to Abolish HUAC. There was little in Frank's early background to suggest that he would ever be a civil liberties activist, or be of any particular interest to the FBI.

He was the fourth and youngest child in a conservative Methodist family. Early in his life, his family moved from his birthplace, Charlevoix, Michigan, to the affluent Los Angeles community of Beverly Hills, where his father established a medical practice. The FBI noted that the senior Wilkinson was a Legionnaire, a past president of the Federated Church Brotherhood, and a well known anti-vice crusader, active in municipal politics.

Frank followed in his father's footsteps, and by high school had become the First President of the Hollywood Young Peoples' Chapter of the Women's Christian Temperance Union. He carried his "dry" politics into the 1932 election, working to save the 18th Amendment through the re-election of President Herbert Hoover.

At UCLA Frank was pledged by SAE, a prestigious fraternity, made the eight-man rowing crew, and became President of the Student Board of the University Religious Conference, an ecumenical group established by the National Conference of Christians and Jews. Winning nomination as the candidate for student body president of the fraternity-sorority caucus, he plunged into campus politics—and civil liberties on the wrong side. His opponent, the nominee of the "non-org" caucus, became embroiled in a petition drive for an open forum on campus, and was expelled by the ultra-conservative Provost.[15] Despite a rising, state-wide student movement in solidarity with the UCLA expellees, Frank came out publicly in support of the expulsions, which conveniently disqualified his opponent. When University of California President Dr. Robert Gordon Sproul overruled his Provost and ordered the students reinstated, Frank lost the election.

Frank's goal was to become a Methodist minister. After graduation at UCLA, before entering divinity school, he planned a trip to Europe and the

Holy Land—a combination religious pilgrimage and romantic journey. In Chicago, he was made suddenly aware of the Depression when he visited Maxwell Street, where he found hungry people grubbing in garbage cans for food. When he eventually reached Jerusalem, he was overwhelmed by the poverty he had seen across the world. His idyllic dreams of visiting the Church of Nativity were shattered by the heart-rending reality of the droves of beggars, the halt, the blind and diseased who blocked the church entrance on Christmas Eve, so he could not enter.

By the time Frank returned to Los Angeles, his old secure conservative world had fallen apart. He was now seeking the New Jerusalem in terms of basic social reform. The FBI was interested enough in his transformation to open up a file. The first entry notes that he had been seen in the company of "known Communists." [16]

By chance, he met Msgr. Thomas O'Dwyer, the Archdiocesan Director of Catholic Charities, who introduced him to slums a few scant miles from his home in Beverly Hills, and recruited him to the Citizens Housing Council, an advocacy group for slum clearance and public housing. From this, it was a logical progression to the staff of the Los Angeles Housing Authority.

As Frank moved up in the Housing Authority, the FBI began to develop the outline of a *neutralization* plan. It determined that the Housing Authority was in part federally financed, providing the rationale for the Bureau's operation.* After Frank campaigned for the integration of the first Watts housing project, he was appointed manager and given the job of implementing the integration he had demanded. As the housing program expanded into a massive $110,000,000 plan for the area, he became the Special Assistant to the Exec-

* An FBI neutralization program to obtain discharge of public employees suspected of radical sympathies was code named RESPONSIBILITIES PROGRAM.[17]

utive Director. Among his new responsibilities was the task of explaining slum clearance and public housing to the general public. This put him in contact with a multitude of groups, ranging from the veterans' organizations and the Catholic, Jewish and Protestant hierarchies to the many diverse community and political groups, including the Communist Party.

In August, 1952, Frank was assigned by the Housing Authority to testify as an expert witness in the condemnation proceedings against a group of property owners in the Chavez Ravine, then a predominantly Hispanic slum. The FBI was well aware of the opposition to the housing plan by real estate groups, articulated by the then conservative *Los Angeles Times*.[18] Here were political allies which the Bureau could utilize to implement its plans. The trap was ready to be sprung.*

The FBI had prepared an alternate plan to go to the governor with Frank's alleged political affiliations.

"Business Address—Unemployed"

Frank testified at length on the slum conditions in the ravine. Came the turn for the opposing counsel. A long and unfriendly cross examination followed. Frank answered in detail those questions he considered proper as an expert witness in such a proceeding. Suddenly he was asked: "Mr. Wilkinson, will you now tell us of all the organizations, political or otherwise, with which you have associated?" The question was clearly irrelevant. It led into the McCarthyite web of guilt by association, a potential entanglement from which there was no exit. Frank refused to answer. The roof fell in.

The story made the next day's headlines in the *Los Angeles Times* and other papers. The court ruled him disqualified as an expert; his testimony was stricken from the record. The Los Angeles City Council, at its next meeting, passed a resolution deploring his refusal to answer and calling upon the House Un-American Activities Committee to come to L.A. to investigate the Housing Authority. Mayor Fletcher Bowron, in self protection, now called upon the State Attorney General to investigate the Authority's personnel.

A stream of telegrams from the FBI Field Office kept Headquarters advised of each new development. California Senate's "little HUAC" supoenaed both Frank and his wife, Jean, a high school social studies teacher, for a closed session. By now it was clear that the hearing's only purpose was the probe of the political associations of persons related to the Housing Authority. As a matter of personal conscience and social responsibility, Frank and Jean felt they had no choice but to refuse to answer. Both were immediately fired from their respective jobs. As the witch-hunt spread in all directions, the Los Angeles housing program collapsed. Chavez Ravine became a ball park.

Frank was unemployable. No employer would touch him with a ten foot pole. The FBI's Security Index form for Frank Wilkinson was updated to record: "Business Address—Unemployed."[19] Finally, Frank found a compassionate Quaker department store owner who agreed to hire him as a night janitor, on condition that he tell no one where he worked. His job was to clean three floors, with sixteen toilets, at a dollar an hour.

The Hollywood YMCA Camp, where the Wilkinson children were scheduled to spend the summer, would allow them to come only on the condition that the parents would not visit them at the Sunday chapel service. "Anything I touch is ruined," Frank confided to a friend. He had been effectively *neutralized*—for the moment.

A New Career

Eventually, Frank got a different kind of job offer. The Hollywood-Los Angeles area, the movie capital of the world, had long been the favorite hunting ground for the House Un-American Activities Committee. In the initial fight-back against HUAC's incursions in 1947, many of Hollywood's celebrities supported the group of subpoenaed screen writers and directors who formed the "Hollywood Ten." Resistance collapsed when the "Ten" failed to win their court battle to use the First Amendment in refusing to answer questions, and were compelled to serve prison sentences. The screen industry's blacklist proceeded to destroy the livelihood of all subsequent HUAC witnesses who refused to "name names." Year after year, HUAC hearings continued, moving from actors to writers to directors to musicians to technicians to carpenters.

To create a new center of resistance, the Rev. A.A. Heist, a retired Methodist minister and director emeritus of the American Civil Liberties Union of Southern California, took the initiative in forming the Citizens Committee to Preserve American Freedoms, dedicated to the single purpose of stopping HUAC. He came to see Frank and asked him to become the Secretary of the new group. It took several meetings to convince Frank that he would not destroy the CCPAF if he took the job.

The CCPAF set out to develop an antidote to HUAC's threefold blitz of *divide, isolate, intimidate.* Each time a new batch of HUAC subpoenas was announced, the CCPAF called an immediate meeting of the subpoenaed persons, before their fears had time to sink in. Constitutional defenses were prepared, legal representation was assured, and immediate plans were made for rallying community support. Confidence and hope were born of solidarity and collective action. A spirit of resistance gathered momentum as sympathetic audiences packed the hearing room and pickets protested outside on the street. Frank gradually rebuilt his own confidence as he saw the growing positive effect of his meticulous organizing.

Dr. Alexander Meiklejohn

In 1955, Senator Thomas Carey Hennings, Jr. of Missouri was named the chair of the Senate Subcommittee on Constitutional Rights. The Senate had censured Senator Joseph McCarthy the year before, and Hennings, a civil libertarian, hoped to create further positive momentum by holding hearings on freedom of speech, press and assembly. As opening witness he invited an eighty-year-old retired educator, Professor Alexander Meiklejohn, nationally respected for his scholarship on the First Amendment.

"Our Citizens Are Sovereign"

Dr. Meiklejohn told the Committee:

> ...The First Amendment seems to me to be a very uncompromising statement. It admits of no exceptions. It tells us that the Congress and, by implication, all other agencies of government are denied any authority whatever to limit the political freedom of the citizens of the United States. It declares that with respect to political belief, political discussion, political advocacy, political planning, our citizens are sovereign, and Congress is their subordinate agent.
>
> ...[N]o subordinate agency of the government has the authority to ask, under compulsion to answer, what a citizen's political commitments are. The question, "Are you a Republican?" or "Are you a

Communist?" when accompanied by the threat of harmful or degrading consequences if an answer is refused, or if the answer is this rather than that, is an intolerable invasion of the "reserved powers" of the governing people. And the freedom thus protected does not rest upon the Fifth Amendment "right" of one who is governed to avoid self-incrimination. It expresses the constitutional authority, the legal power, of one who governs to make up his own mind without fear or favor...

As he was preparing a mass meeting to protest a HUAC hearing in 1956, Frank called Dr. Meiklejohn at his home in Berkeley to invite him to repeat his Hennings Committee testimony in Los Angeles. Meiklejohn readily accepted. So began a collaboration which would continue until Meiklejohn's death eight years later. Meiklejohn's First Amendment position became the cornerstone of the movement to abolish HUAC.

Dr. Alexander Meiklejohn was a gentle scholar and educator whose penetrating social criticisms made him a controversial figure throughout his long career. Dean at Brown College (1903-11), president of Amherst (1912-23), chair of the Experimental College at Wisconsin (1927-32), and founder of the San Francisco School of Social Studies (1933-41), his innovative ideas left an indelible mark on generations of students he taught and inspired. His mind encompassed the human situation as a whole, not permitting academic discipline to splinter his thinking.

While serving on the ACLU National Board (1927-63), he developed a distinct, historically based interpretation of the First Amendment, which in a voluminous correspondence he shared with the justices of the Supreme Court.

In the last year of his eventful life, Dr. Meiklejohn was nominated by President John F.

Kennedy for the Presidential Medal of Freedom. It was presented by President Lyndon B. Johnson in a White House ceremony in 1963.

HUAC Subpoenas Wilkinson

At 7 A.M. in the morning after the mass meeting at which Meiklejohn spoke, Wilkinson was subpoenaed to appear before HUAC. When he appeared at the hearing, he was represented by ACLU legal counsel A.L. Wirin, who was prepared to help him make a constitutional test case of Meiklejohn's First Amendment thesis.

The FBI followed the hearing closely. ▨▨▨▨▨ ▨▨▨▨▨▨▨▨▨▨▨▨▨▨▨▨▨▨ * a HUAC staff member reported to the Bureau:

> Throughout the course of the questioning which ensued, Wilkinson refused to answer any questions and though he invoked the First Amendment, he pointedly refused to invoke the Fifth...At the conclusion of his testimony, Congressman Gordon Scherer moved that Wilkinson be cited for contempt, at which time all members voted affirmatively...[20]

Ultimately, to Frank's surprise, the full committee** decided not to cite him at this time.*** [21] Two years later, in July, 1958, Frank was invited to Atlanta, Georgia, by the Southern Conference Educational Fund (SCEF), an inter-racial civil rights group, to assist a group of civil rights activists who had been subpoenaed for a HUAC hearing. When Frank arrived in Atlanta, just a week before the hearing, he was met at the door of his hotel room by a U.S. Marshall with a HUAC subpoena.

Frank's Atlanta journey was known, as far as he knew, only to the SCEF people who had called him, and a few close associates. Otherwise, only someone with access to his private communica-

* Gray bars as used here and hereafter in the text refer to names and/or other identifying characteristics of non-public figure third persons which have been deleted pursuant to a protective order entered in Frank Wilkinson et al v. FBI et al, U.S. District Court, Central District of California, Case No. CV 80-1048 AWT (Tx).

** Anita Belle Schneider, prior to Wilkinson being called to the witness stand, testified that she knew him as a communist. The decision not to cite Wilkinson at that time was doubtless based upon advice from the FBI that Schneider was an unreliable witness, who might have been called by the defense if the trial were held in Los Angeles. By the time of the Atlanta trial, the FBI did not know her whereabouts.[22]

*** The Immigration and Naturalization Service asked the FBI for a search of records on the *chance that Wilkinson might be foreign born and deportable. For the INS, this was apparently a Standing Operating Procedure for "unfriendly" HUAC witnesses - one of the concrete ways in which this agency played a supportive role in political witch-hunts. The INS thought that he might be a Communist Party candidate for public office in Canada in 1932. Wilkinson was actually campaigning at the time for Herbert Hoover.* 23

tions could have had advance warning—like the FBI, which was spinning a new web to *neutralize* him.

For a second time, Frank stood on his First Amendment Rights in refusing to answer all questions. He was legally represented this time by the National ACLU. Carl Braden, a civil rights veteran and staff worker for SCEF, took a similar stand. Both were cited for contempt on August 13, 1958 and tried and convicted in the Atlanta District Court on January 22, 1959. The FBI followed every step of their cases up the appellate ladder to the U.S. Supreme Court.[24]

On his way home to Los Angeles, Frank stopped over in Montgomery, Alabama, to consult with Aubrey Williams, SCEF president. A month later, Williams accepted an invitation to come to Los Angeles to address an anti-HUAC rally. After learning that Dr. Meiklejohn and Robert Kenny, a former California Attorney General, were committed to the crusade to abolish HUAC, Aubrey agreed to join the team. As Chairperson of the National Committee, Aubrey was destined to play a decisive role.

Aubrey Williams

Aubrey Williams had his own reasons for opposing the congressional inquisitorial committees. A social worker who had won national prominence as a crusader against poverty and racial segregation, he was recruited in the formative years of Roosevelt's New Deal Administration to help develop an emergency program for twenty million workers who were jobless and destitute. When Harry Hopkins was made director of the Works Project Administration, the primary job creating agency, Aubrey Williams served as his deputy, as well as director of the National Youth Administration, which provided jobs and training for some five million unemployed young people.

His hard driving social commitment, and his pioneering efforts in the deep South to buck the established patterns of racial segregation, attracted the attention of Eleanor Roosevelt. Aubrey became an intimate of the White House circle. With the death of FDR, and the advent of the Cold War, the Old Boys' segregationist network in the South and his anti-New Deal enemies in the North ultimately drove him out of government service. HUAC's Senate counterpart, the Senate Internal Security Subcommittee (SISS) and the FBI played their part.

Williams was called before a SISS hearing in New Orleans in 1954. Although he denied under oath that he had been a member of the Communist Party and answered all questions, it availed him little. It was his word against an array of FBI informers. Whittaker Chambers* had testified earlier that he was known as "a friend of the Communist Party." John Butler also a former Communist, stated that Aubrey was introduced to him in 1942 as "Comrade Williams." Paul Crouch, another leading performer on the informer circuit, testified that Aubrey was introduced to him by a prominent Communist as a "chief national leader", who was a "secret member." Aubrey admitted to the Subcommittee that he had defended the right of a Communist to hold a job; and that he was the president of SCEF, which HUAC had cited as a "Communist Front."[24]

*Perhaps the most infamous of the ex-Communist FBI informers, with his "pumpkin papers," Whittaker Chambers was instrumental in the conviction of Alger Hiss for perjury. He was awarded a posthumous Medal of Freedom by Ronald Reagan, while his farm has been declared an Historical Monument by Secretary of Interior Hodel, over-ruling the unanimous negative recommendation of the advisory committee.

Forced out of government work, Williams established a successful printing and newspaper business in his old home town of Montgomery, Alabama. He was one of the few prominent Southern whites to publicly support the Montgomery bus boycott and the subsequent civil rights struggles, winning the friendship and confidence of Reverend Martin Luther King, Jr. and the leadership of the Southern Christian Leadership Conference. But the South was a fertile field for red-baiting, which was used by his political enemies to undermine his business. He still retained the friendship of many of his New Deal associates, including Eleanor Roosevelt, and was able to enlist their support for the abolition of HUAC. When Aubrey became the Chairperson of the newly formed National Committee to Abolish HUAC he provided a vital connection with influential liberal circles in Washington and with the emerging national civil rights movement.

HUAC Hearing In San Francisco

HUAC's own actions in 1960 did much to inadvertently set the stage for the launching of a national movement for its abolition. In May of 1960, HUAC opened hearings in San Francisco to pillory a group of Northern California Communist leaders, and some alleged Communists including an undergraduate student at the University of California in Berkeley. Student activism in the area was coming alive with a focus on civil liberties and the emerging civil rights struggles in the South.* Prior to the San Francisco hearings, HUAC harassment of California teachers had stirred hostile feelings among students, many of whom planned teaching careers. Hundreds of Berkeley students decided to attend the hearings. Frightened by the prospect of an unsympathetic audience, the HUAC staff tried to ensure a friendly gallery by issuing special passes to members of conservative fundamentalist churches, American Legion posts and other centers of anti-communist persuasion.

When the doors opened, only a few of the long

* Students there, as elsewhere in the country, were inspired by the struggles of Black students in the South, who earlier that year launched the sit-ins which, as part of the civil rights movement, were destined to change the South forever. As some Berkeley students said later, "We decided that if Black students in the South could do what they were doing, we could do something, too." [Note from Anne Braden based upon her 1960 interviews with Berkeley students.]

San Francisco City Hall staircase as police use firehoses to remove student protestors who had been promised "first come, first served" admission to HUAC Hearings, May 13, 1960. --*S.F. Examiner*

line of waiting students were admitted. With mounting indignation, they watched as late arrivals, with special passes, pushed ahead to be admitted to the hearing room. During the noon recess, the San Francisco sheriff promised that they would be admitted "first come, first served" to the afternoon session. But again, they waited in vain as the carriers of special passes were ushered into the hearing room. At this point, the students began to protest vocally. The police, in turn, pulled a fire-hose off the wall, and fired it, full blast, into the crowd of students. Soon the classic rotunda of the City Hall was awash with struggling students and club-swinging police. The great staircase became a waterfall as hundreds of bodies were hauled and pushed down the slippery stairs. Sixty-eight students were dragged out to waiting paddy wagons. In subsequent trials, all were found "not guilty" of the assorted charges.

By the next day's hearing, thousands of students poured into the San Francisco Civic Center from Berkeley, Stanford, and a dozen other nearby colleges, to demonstrate against HUAC. By the time it returned to Washington, the House Committee had many enemies in the Bay area.*

*Two members of Congress, Don Edwards and Phil Burton, who were to play decisive roles in the abolition of HUAC, were elected from the area in the next election.

"Operation Abolition"

To try to reverse a tide of adverse opinion, HUAC undertook the unprecedented action of going into the movie-making business. It subpoenaed the newsreel film clips of the hearing, and made a composite "documentary," with interviews with the HUAC Congressmen before a staged backdrop of the Capitol dome, and a commentary written by Fulton Lewis III, a HUAC staff member and son of right-wing columnist and commentator Fulton

Lewis, Jr. Entitled "Operation Abolition," the film came under heavy attack for a number of clearly identifiable distortions of fact and alterations of sequence. An editorial in the *Washington Post* on 11/26/60 dubbed it a "forgery by film", and a number of respected journals, including the *Christian Century*, published highly critical analyses.

Frank Wilkinson, who had gone to San Francisco to witness the hearing, make contact with community leaders, and distribute an initial speech by Representative Roosevelt critical of HUAC, was cast in the film as one of the villains, along with labor leader, Harry Bridges, though neither played more than an observer role. Nonetheless, ▒▒▒▒▒▒▒▒▒▒▒▒▒▒▒▒▒▒▒▒▒▒▒▒▒ a HUAC staff member advised the FBI that Wilkinson was "one of the principal organizers in resisting the HCUA hearings." On the basis of this report, the Los Angeles Field Office recommended to Headquarters: "In view of the fact that Wilkinson has exhibited considerable ability as a disruptionist, it is recommended that he be tabbed for Detcom," (a political equivalent of the "ten most wanted," scheduled for first internment in case of a national emergency).[25]

With no independent investigation of its own, the FBI Crime Records Division used the HUAC version of the hearings for a pamphlet, "Communist Target—Youth," with J. Edgar Hoover officially listed as the author. Frank Wilkinson was featured as the chief "disruptionist."

Produced at government expense, "Operation Abolition" was sold to a private film distributor, which did a lucrative business selling 500 copies to large corporations and pro-HUAC groups.[26] When shown to business executives and other captive audiences, often with an appropriate accompanying lecture, it was effective in propagating the central theme that the San Francisco disorders were instigated by a "Communist" plot, with gullible students acting as dupes.

On college campuses, however, where it was shown from coast to coast, it backfired. The pictures of students, men and women alike, knocked about by high pressure hose and police riot sticks antagonized most student audiences. When students were told by Congressmen Gordon Scherer and August Johansen that they were "toying with treason," when they questioned HUAC, many students were ready to join a local student committee to abolish HUAC.

Representative James Roosevelt, representing a south Los Angeles district, had been actively lobbied by his district to speak out against HUAC. After the San Francisco hearings, he delivered a new indictment of the House Committee, which was reprinted and widely distributed by the National Committee to Abolish HUAC. In it, Roosevelt promised to move, on the opening day of the next Congress, to rescind HUAC's mandate. A dramatic public action would be needed to back his initiative.

Frank Wilkinson came to New York City on November 17, 1960, to attend a meeting of the newly formed New York Council to Abolish HUAC—a local affiliate of the National Committee. Fresh from meetings on college campuses, he was convinced that students would respond to a national mobilization against HUAC in Washington, timed with the opening of the new Congress. He proposed a combination mass demonstration and lobby for January 2, 1961.

Among those present was   of the Bronx Civil Liberties Committee, an undercover informer for the FBI. His message was relayed by the SAC (Special Agent-in-Charge), New York by AIRTEL to the Director.

American Nazi Party counter-
pickets, Washington, D.C.,
January, 1961.

... source advised that plans were discussed for a mass picket demonstration to be held at the White House...on January 2, between noon and 2 P.M... New York will strive to have 300 individuals participate...[27]

Pickets For HUAC

At Headquarters, wheels began to turn. Memos were prepared for the Attorney General and Major General William B. Persons, assistant to the President. Field offices were alerted. Soon reports of student mobilization plans, some wildly exaggerated, were coming in from Chicago, San Francisco, St. Louis, Boston, Philadelphia, Wisconsin and Michigan.[28] Memos were dispatched to Washington intelligence and law enforcement agencies— the Secret Service, Military intelligence agencies, U.S. Park Police, the Metropolitan Police Department, and the Military District of Washington, which was mandated to keep "a representative number of troops under arms," presumably in case the student pickets should decide to assault the White House.

In early December, the New York Council to Abolish HUAC sent out a mailing to 10,000, calling for support and participation in the Washington action. The mailing was an amalgam of borrowed lists of potential supporters. It included the subscription list of the Communist *Worker.* The public relations department of the ▓▓▓▓▓ Co. was a subscriber, and an alert employee noticed that the addressograph plates for the N.Y. Council mailing and the *Worker* wrappers were similar. After talking to an FBI agent friend, he mailed his exhibits to the head of the N.Y. Field Office, who in turn fired them off to FBI Headquarters, with a memo noting their potential as "a counterintelligence measure." "It would be very damaging," he wrote the Director, "if it were known that the New York Council to Abolish HUAC was using the facilities of a Communist newspaper to disseminate its propaganda." [29]

The FBI Lab confirmed that the two addresses were indeed printed from the same addressograph plate. To reach the public in time to damage the anti-HUAC mobilization, Headquarters rushed the material out to its confidential media outlets. In his summary of successful COINTELPRO operations, the FBI Supervisor noted:

> Through the efforts of the Crime Records Division, Fulton Lewis, the well known commentator, exposed this tie-up on his radio program on 12/28/60. In addition, HCUA put out a special wire service release on 12/28/60 exposing the above situation.[30]

Spurred by the adverse publicity and the "Communist" label pinned on the January 2, 1961 anti-HUAC demonstration, a variety of right-wing groups began organizing counter-demonstrations. Heavily censored FBI documents suggest that some of the organizers of the counter-demonstrations were old friends of FBI officials. Field offices continued to send in last minute information from their informers and wiretaps.[31]

The Washington Field Office prepared detailed plans for surveillance of the White House demonstration and the related gatherings of the National Committee to Abolish HUAC. The Los Angeles office provided five current photos of Wilkinson to facilitate physical surveillance. Contact was established with the management of the ▓▓▓▓▓ Hotel, where Wilkinson had reserved ten rooms for National Committee leaders. The management readily provided the FBI with the list of those who registered for these rooms.

The Metropolitan Police Department summarized the participation in the demonstration as follows:[32]

Pro-HUAC

Number:

21 American Nazi Party, 17 males in uniform with swastika arm bands, 4 females.

Signs carried:

God Bless Congressman Walter

Only Jews and Communists Oppose HCUA

7 Fighting American Nationalists (offshoot of ANP)

140 Anti-Communist International (mostly Hungarian & Cuban refugees)

120 Young Americans for Freedom

Anti-HUAC

212 Students who came by New York bus.

Note: Other students and representatives from other states not recorded.

After visiting congressional offices, the anti-HUAC demonstrators were bused to Pierce Hall, All Souls Unitarian Church, to hear talks by Aubrey Williams; Willard Uphaus, a distinguished Methodist layman who had just served a year in jail in New Hampshire for refusing to give the state "little HUAC" a list of registrants at World Fellowship summer camp; Burton White, a University of California graduate student who had been hosed, clubbed and arrested at the San Francisco hearings; and Sandra Rosenblum, the executive secretary of the New York Youth Council.

Outside, some 200 pro-HUAC picketers—Hungarians and Cubans who had been bused in from New York, along with a sprinkling of Young Americans for Freedom—were yelling anti-Communist slogans and milling about. Captain Michael Mahaney of the MPD expressed some concerns about potential violence outside and complimented the gathering for its disciplined and peaceful conduct.*

"Can We Expedite That?"

On February 27, 1961, the U.S. Supreme Court handed down its decision upholding the convictions of Wilkinson and Braden. Justice Potter Stewart wrote the decision for the majority. Four justices, Black, Douglas, Brennan and Chief Justice Warren dissented. Black, Douglas and Brennan wrote separate dissenting opinions.

To quote Justice Black:

> In my view, the majority by its decision today places the stamp of constitutional approval upon a practice as clearly inconsistent with the Constitution, and indeed with every ideal of individual freedom for which this county has so long stood as any that has ever come before this Court ... [T]his case involves nothing more or less than an attempt by the Un-American Activities Committee to use the contempt power of the House of Representatives as a weapon against those who dare to criticize it ... This Country was not built by men who were afraid and it cannot be preserved by such men.

The FBI had been impatiently awaiting the high court's decision. Now that it had spoken, they were furious that Wilkinson was still "touring the country attacking HCUA." A staff memo states: "...the specific date he will report to begin service of his sentence will depend upon receipt by the lower court of the Supreme Court mandate." "CAN WE EXPEDITE THAT?" Hoover wrote across the bottom of the memo.[34]

By requesting a rehearing, Frank won a brief respite. He was scheduled to address a student meeting on the Berkeley campus on March 22. A

* The Metropolitan Police Department was less pleased with the conduct of the Secret Service and The U.S. Park Police at the demonstration, who, without consulting with the MPD, had taken the provocative action of calling for fire fighting equipment. The Deputy Chief of the MPD countermanded the order.[33]

group of fundamentalist preachers and right-wing state legislators, with help from Hearst's San Francisco Examiner, were stirring up a storm of protest against his speaking. Berkeley State Assembly member Don Mulford demanded that University President Clark Kerr bar this "FBI labeled pro-Communist agitator" from the campus, and outlaw SLATE, the student sponsoring group.

Chancellor Adrian Kragen, pleading the University's policy of "hearing both sides", tried to placate the protesters by inviting an FBI speaker to respond to Wilkinson. The local FBI referred the question to Headquarters which declined the invitation on grounds of "short notice."

Privately, J. Edgar Hoover was not so polite. "I am absolutely opposed to this crowd of 'bleeding hearts' at Berkeley using the FBI to get off the hook," he noted. "I know Kerr is no good and I doubt Kragen is."[35]

Five thousand Berkeley students turned out to hear Wilkinson, overflowing Wheeler Auditorium. Loudspeakers were rigged to reach the thousands outside. Frank concluded his address with the words: "We will not save free speech if we are not prepared to go to jail in its defense. I am prepared to pay that price." The auditorium exploded with a standing ovation.

Joined by his co-defendant Carl Braden, Frank made a fast tour across country, speaking to large and sympathetic audiences at every stop. FBI efforts to get meetings cancelled and to plant derogatory news stories were ineffective. Their last night of freedom was spent at a reception hosted by a group of civil rights leaders which included the Rev. Martin Luther King, Jr. and Aubrey Williams. Seventeen, including King, signed a plea to President Kennedy to free Braden and Wilkinson,

Dr. Martin Luther King, Jr., Frank Wilkinson, Carl Braden, and Dr. James Dombrowski, at reception sponsored by the Southern Christian Leadership Conference to honor Braden and Wilkinson on the occasion of their surrender to federal authorities to commence their prison sentences for their First Amendment defiance of HUAC, Morehouse College, Atlanta, Georgia, April 30, 1961.

Frank Wilkinson and Carl Braden behind bars at Fulton County Jail, Atlanta, Georgia, May 1, 1961.

which provided the foundation for a Southern petition for clemency.

There Are No Political Prisoners—We Just Treat Them Differently

On May 1, 1961, Frank and Carl reported to federal authorities to begin serving their sentences. They became the immediate objects of extraordinary surveillance. After a brief stay in the Atlanta jail, they were shipped to the Federal Prison Camp at Donaldson Airforce Base in Greenville, North Carolina. The FBI Field Office in Charlotte was instructed to contact prison officials for information regarding Frank Wilkinson as to "... possible duration of his imprisonment at FCI, Greenville; his morale, attitude and condition of health; correspondence and volume of mail thus far received; prison employment, etc."[36]

The FBI briefed the Bureau of Prisons personnel on the alleged Communist affiliations of Braden and Wilkinson to ensure that prison rules would be rigidly enforced.

When Aubrey Williams and his wife, Anita, drove all the way up from Montgomery, Alabama to see Frank and Carl, they were denied permission, even though Aubrey had been an associate of Director of Prisons William W. Bennett.

Special arrangements were made for the parole officer to provide the FBI with copies of all incoming and outgoing correspondence. Although Wilkinson was eligible for parole after serving one third of his sentence, enjoyed an unblemished prison record, and had no prior arrest beyond a traffic ticket, parole was never seriously considered. By the time that Frank and Carl had adjusted well to Greenville and had gained many friends among the inmates, they were suddenly transferred to Allenwood, Pa. The official explanation was that the presence of Frank and Carl endangered the security of the adjacent airforce base. They were put on a prison bus for the long, uncomfortable ride, first to the main prison at Lewisburg for reprocessing and then to the Allenwood prison camp.

The FBI found that there were no copying facilities at Allenwood. Arrangements had to be quickly improvised to use the equipment at Lewisburg in such a way that Frank and Carl "would not be aware of any delay in the handling of their mail." [37]

The FBI apparently counted on Frank's imprisonment to undermine the anti-HUAC movement in two ways. Depriving the National Committee of the man they considered to be the "brains and energy" of the organization might cause it to fall apart.[38] Second, it planned to use Frank's prison record to undermine his acceptability as a public speaker.

Petitions For Amnesty

Ironically, the Supreme Court's decision actually spurred the abolition movement. The powerful dissenting opinions gave credibility to the National Committee's First Amendment stand against HUAC. With its adoption of the Wilkinson case, the American Civil Liberties Union had moved into more active support of the abolition of HUAC. The imprisonment of Wilkinson and Braden acted as a call-to-arms for civil libertarians.

The New York Council to Abolish HUAC launched a petition drive to the President for executive clemency. A separate national petition, initiated by Clarence Pickett, Director Emeritus of the American Friends Service Committee, and coordinated by New York activist and historian, Sylvia

Crane, enlisted a distinguished group of religious and academic leaders. Through the combined efforts of Crane and the Chicago Committee to Defend the Bill of Rights, it was mailed to ten thousand opinion makers in professional fields. More than three thousand responded. They were joined by parliamentary leaders in Great Britain, France and other Western European countries.* As the names of the signers were collected by the Chicago Field Office, they were reported to FBI Headquarters and immediately sent to field offices across the country to be "indexed."[39] A major sector of the nation's intellectual elite were, unknown to them, being placed in the FBI's subversive files.

*One signer was Francois Mitterand, then Socialist Deputy, now President of the French Republic.

Meanwhile in the South, SCEF was conducting a major educational drive around the circulation of the petition for clemency which had been initiated on the day that Carl and Frank went to prison in Atlanta, ultimately enlisting the support of thousands of signers throughout the South. Rev. Wyatt Tee Walker, executive director of the Southern Christian Leadership Conference took time out from the pressing demands of the civil rights movement to assist SCEF in organizing an influential 18-member delegation to present the petitions at the White House. Other top aides of the Rev. Martin Luther King, Jr., the Revs. Ralph Abernathy and Fred Shuttlesworth, played major roles in the petition campaign.

Carl Braden's wife, Anne, travelled the South, talking to groups about the dangers of HUAC to the integrationist movement, and distributing a SCEF pamphlet she had written. In October, SCEF sponsored a major conference on "Freedom and the First Amendment" in Chapel Hill, NC, which attracted Black and White participation from 11 Southern states. Thus, by the time that Frank and Carl were released from prison, there was a large body of opinion within the Southern civil rights movement, especially among students, who viewed opposition to HUAC as an integral part of their own struggle.

In August, the New York petition was ready for presentation to the White House and the Pardon Attorney of the Department of Justice by a small delegation headed by Frank's wife, Jean. To discourage a friendly reception, Hoover had memos hand delivered to both offices. In November, the VIP petition was to be presented by a group of prominent theologians and civil rights leaders. Thanks to a wiretap on the phone of a Washington Area Committee member involved in the arrangements, the Washington Field Office learned that a White House aide scheduled to receive the petition was rumored to be sympathetic to the petitioners. Again, the Director rushed memos to the White House and arranged to "orally" deliver the "delicate" information concerning the aide.[40]

The petition campaign failed to free Frank and Carl. The FBI won the battle, but lost the war. Wilkinson and Braden emerged from prison as nationally recognized leaders.

They were due for release, with credit for "good time," on February 1, 1962. Frank was informed by his parole officer that he would be free to leave at 8 AM, furnished with transportation to New York City. The New York Field Office, however, took note of the preparations for a large "welcome home" rally in New York's St. Nicholas Arena, which it reported to the Director. Shortly thereafter, the Allenwood prison officials made a sudden change of plans. Frank and Carl were held until late afternoon of their day of freedom, and then put on a bus to Los Angeles. Thanks to the solidarity of the prisoners, Frank learned of the switch through the prison grapevine, and managed to send word to New York. Accordingly, a car was dispatched to intercept the bus at its first stop, and race back to New York City. Six hundred people at the Arena waited for two-and-a-half-hours, while Pete Seeger led a sing along. At 10:30 Frank made a dramatic entrance.

For the next months, Frank and Carl were in great demand. An FBI Headquarters memo records:

Both Braden and Wilkinson are Security Index subjects. Since their release for contempt of Congress, they have traveled extensively in carrying out their program toward the abolition of the House Committee on Un-American Activities. They have been treated as heroes and martyrs by the communist and subversive groups they have appeared before.[41]

The FBI continued to write its defamatory "blind memos" on Wilkinson and Braden, which Cartha DeLoach distributed surreptitiously to his media contacts, but it was not enough to stop the gathering momentum of the abolish HUAC drive.

Disruptive Tactics

On April 30, 1962, the neutralization program against NCAHUAC entered a new phase of physical activism. The Director sent a directive to the eight field offices covering Frank's scheduled speaking tour. These orders were to be repeated each time Wilkinson undertook a speaking tour during the next five years.

Offices receiving instant communication are instructed to be alert for counterintelligence operations which might be effectively employed concerning these various speaking engagements of Wilkinson. Any operations that could be employed as a disruptive tactic should be furnished the Bureau setting forth complete details regard-

> ing the proposed operation; however, such an operation should not be placed in effect without specific Bureau authorization.[42]

A month earlier, Special Agent [redacted], in charge of the COINTELPRO in the Minneapolis Field Office, had provided a model "disruptive tactic." Using the services of [redacted], a one-time paid informer who had infiltrated the Democratic Farmer Labor Party (DFL), he manipulated the labor leadership into cancelling the contract to use the Labor Temple for a Wilkinson meeting. The denial of the hall, coupled with a barrage of news stories citing Wilkinson's alleged communist ties, was deemed by Headquarters "a completely successful disruption." The Director subsequently gave SA [redacted] the "Incentive Award".[43]

In Washington, D.C. a special agent disguised as an "inquiring reporter" appeared at the door of the All Souls Unitarian Church where Wilkinson and Braden were to speak. As people were about to enter, he asked names and addresses and such questions as "why are you attending?", "do you know Frank Wilkinson?" Not surprisingly, some turned around and left. As the field office memo noted, Washington "is a particularly sensitive area with regard to publicity for organizations in opposition to HUAC."[44]

In Chicago, the field office apologized to Headquarters for the lack of effective measures against Wilkinson which could be instituted "at this late date." However, the field office was developing a "disruptive tactic" to undermine the work of the Chicago Committee to Defend the Bill of Rights, the midwest office for the National Committee. A letter signed *"True believers in democratic and constitutional process"* was sent to Board members urging the dismissal of Richard Criley, the Executive Secretary, alleging he was a secret Stalinist whose "motives" were suspect.[45] Most Board members deposited the anonymous mailing in the waste basket. But one member quietly resigned.

The letter was later mailed to an anti-communist Jewish publication, to bring pressure on two rabbis on the Board. It was then sent to Illinois State Senator Broyles, the author of a number of anti-communist bills, in hopes that he might investigate the Chicago Committee. Neither move produced "tangible results."

In Cleveland, Criley and Wilkinson were scheduled to appear as guests on the Mike Douglas TV "call in" show. ASAC [Ass't Agent-in-Charge] ▨▨▨▨▨ ▨▨▨▨▨▨▨▨▨ was authorized to see his contact at KYW-TV who "was most anxious to cooperate with the Bureau in any way possible ... [N]o other employees at the television station would be aware of the Bureau's interest." The Los Angeles and Chicago Field Offices were asked to draft embarrassing questions to be asked the two studio guests. "Public Source" data was dispatched to Cleveland. It turned out that Criley did not make the trip and Wilkinson's TV appearance was reduced to a ten-minute taped interview, in which some of the FBI prepared script was used.

That afternoon Wilkinson addressed a group at the Jewish Cultural Center in Cleveland. As its special agent for disruption, the FBI utilized Mrs. Leta Wood and her "Organization to Fight Communism." The FBI memo notes:

This meeting was picketed by approximately 15-20 persons, each carrying a placard stating, "We like HCUA," "Wilkinson is a Communist" and "HCUA—yes, Wilkinson—no." ... The picketing ... apparently attracted a number of teenagers, who were so noisy that the doors and windows of the hall were closed, and that hall became unbearably warm. The custodian turned on what he believed to be the air-conditioning unit, but which was the furnace, and after half an hour, it was necessary to open the doors. The teenagers then came into the back of the hall and heckled the speaker ...[46]

These examples of creative disruptions in Cleveland were disseminated to 15 field offices by the Director. Special precautions, however, were taken to restrict knowledge of COINTELPRO within the FBI itself. "Each SAC [Special Agent in Charge] receiving this letter is instructed to have only those Agents assigned to the Counterintelligence Program read this letter and after it has been thoroughly read it should be personally destroyed by the SAC and the Bureau advised that it has been so destroyed."[47]

As the 1962 fall term of colleges and universities began, Wilkinson focused his tour on reaching student audiences. While repeating his exhortations to the field offices to "give careful consideration to possible counterintelligence plans to disrupt the efforts of Wilkinson ...", the Director cautioned: "Since Wilkinson's speaking engagements are scheduled to be held on College campuses, the utmost discretion will be necessary to avoid any possible basis for allegations that the Bureau is interfering with academic freedom."[48]

Despite the FBI's redoubled efforts to disrupt his fall tour, most of Wilkinson's meetings were successful. He and Carl Braden scored a victory at Wayne State University, where a May meeting, through FBI intervention, had been denied. The university president now reversed himself and authorized their campus appearance.

Only in Minnesota, under the leadership of Agent ■■■■■, were the "disruptive tactics" partially effective. The scheduled Wilkinson meeting at Macalester College was cancelled by the faculty, thanks to the FBI's covert intervention. At the University of Minnesota, ex-FBI paid informer ▓▓▓▓ ▓▓▓▓ again used ▓▓▓ influence with the Democratic Farmer Labor Party leadership to force the DFL Youth Club to withdraw its sponsorship of the Wilkinson meeting. Before it could be cancelled, however, the student club of the Americans for Democratic Action stepped in to take over sponsorship. The persistent ▓▓▓▓▓ was still able to upset Wilkinson with red-baiting questions from the floor.[49]

Efforts to disrupt Wilkinson's meeting at Knox College, Illinois, failed. Although the FBI hand delivered "blind memos" on Frank just prior to Texas Republican Senator Tower's speaking date at Knox, Tower failed to mention Wilkinson or HUAC.[50] Finally, it was arranged to have Ex-HUAC-staffer Fulton Lewis III invited to speak at Knox (for a handsome honorarium).

Dubious Allies

One effect of the April 30, 1962 directive was the increasing aggressiveness of neutralization efforts. Where meetings could not be cancelled, the FBI relied increasingly on anti-communist organizations including the American Legion, the Young Americans for Freedom, and local groups like Leta Wood's Ohio "Organization to Fight Communism." The FBI was not averse to utilizing even neo-Nazis, as long as the FBI's involvement was sufficiently indirect to be secure from exposure. With such groups, FBI control was limited or non-existent.

A meeting at American University in Washington, D.C. is illustrative. On this occasion, the Washington Field Office made contact with AU officials "to cause cancellation or otherwise disrupt the meeting." The Field Office report on the Washington Area Committee to Abolish HUAC states what happened,

The WACAHUAC meeting featuring **James For-man, Aubrey Williams,** and **Frank Wilkinson** as speakers was held on October 10, 1963, at AU. Approximately 500 people, mostly students, were present. It was originally planned that WACA-HUAC would collect admissions at the door but AU authorities would not allow this. They did, however, underwrite the expenses connected with this meeting place and agreed to an honorarium for **Forman**.

School officials also would not permit WACA-HUAC representatives to be stationed at the entrance to keep possible troublemakers out. They said the meeting was open to all. [My emphasis]

Aubrey Williams was introduced as the first speaker but was unable to complete his speech due to heckling by members of the ANP (American Nazi Party] several of whom were ejected by the police.

Frank Wilkinson was the second speaker and gave a lengthy address, stressing the need for abolition of the HCUA ....

Wilkinson was also heckled by ANP members and at one point was attacked on the platform by a young woman who clawed and scratched at him. This woman and several other individuals were ejected during **Wilkinson's** speech.[51]

The FBI was keenly aware that the Washington Committee, like the National Committee, was having financial difficulties and had borrowed money to cover advance expenses of the meeting. The University's decision not to permit admission fees was a serious blow to the local committee's finances. The granting of an honorarium to James Forman, but not the National Committee speakers, was part of the same calculated policy. The refusal to exclude known violent disrupters and to virtually welcome the thugs from the ANP could not have been accidental, since the FBI kept close track of ANP activities.

The FBI report minimized the violence and the injury to Frank Wilkinson, who was kicked in the groin, as well as scratched and clawed by the female Nazi. A later FBI report from Chicago described his injury, which forced him to lecture sitting down.[52]

On October 13, three days after his AU meeting, his appearance before the Cleveland Unitarian Society also was violently disrupted, this time by Leta Wood and her followers.

Sometimes the work of the FBI's accomplices was counter-productive.

On May 5, 1964, Wilkinson's invitation to speak before the Humanist Society of Toledo, Ohio, University was attacked by the Lucas County Council of the American Legion. The night before the meeting, the Legion passed a resolution condemning the President and Trustees of the University for permitting Wilkinson to speak there. The concluding resolve read:

Be It Further RESOLVED, that we call on students from the University and citizens of this area to shun this Communist Party member and to express abhorrence at this invitation by not attending ...

Copies of the Legion resolution, widely distributed on campus, had the effect of publicizing an otherwise obscure meeting sponsored by a small organization. The attendance of 80 to 100 was undoubtedly in excess of what the attendance would have been without the Legion's heavy handed publicity. The campus newspaper described the opening of the meeting:

The Lucas County Council of the American Legion had passed a resolution condemning Mr. Wilkinson's appearance the day before he arrived, and publicized it extensively to urge a boycott of the meeting.

Before Mr. Wilkinson began his address, he requested one of the campus police officers in attendance to bring an American flag to the auditorium. The officer was unable to find a flag in the Snyder Building.

"Please do not misunderstand my request, or make fun of the officer" he said. "In the light of the reception I thought I should make the request." ... He expressed his gratitude to those who chose to disregard the boycott and attend the meeting.[53]

The Bureau's continuing neutralization efforts continued through the end of 1966. Throughout this entire period, the April 30, 1962 directive to disrupt Wilkinson's meetings accompanied every memo detailing his speaking schedules. A Los Angeles airtel dated 11/17/66 to Albuquerque, Omaha and San Antonio noted, "attention is called to prior Bureau instructions that offices be alert for counterintelligence operations..."

As the National Committee's efforts gained support in the House of Representatives, the Bureau's political reporting increased, providing the House Un-American Activities staff director with the details of the Congressional resolutions and strategies being prepared by opposition Representatives Don Edwards, Phil Burton and others.

"Our Relations With HUAC Have Been Strained"

These Bureau activities were suddenly interrupted by a change of policy announced in a Headquarters Memo dated 1/4/67, to Assistant Director W.C. Sullivan:*

The FBI's covert relations with HUAC were eventually resumed.[54]

> In view of the fact that our relations with the House Committee on Un-American Activities have

been strained and the Director has instructed that no contact be made with it, it is recommended that the above information regarding Wilkinson's proposed trip not be furnished to the House Committee on Un-American Activities. You will be kept advised of pertinent developments regarding this matter.[55]

The change of attitude toward HUAC coincided with a sudden dropping off of the *neutralization* program against the National Committee. There is only one further clear example of a counterintelligence operation, in which the National Committee was an incidental target. Captioned COINTELPRO-NEW LEFT, it describes a forged flier used in 1970 in a Boston operation against two "New Left" student peace groups, the Student Mobilization Committee and the Progressive Labor faction of the Students for a Democratic Society, which used the return address of the National Committee's mail box.[56]

The FBI's Network Of Accomplices

* The ACLU Washington Director in 1958 met with an FBI contact for confidential exchanges of information. "He remarked that recently he saw an individual by the name of Frank Wilkinson of Los Angeles . . . over on the Hill . . . He was surprised to learn that Wilkinson was on his way to the office of Congressman James Roosevelt . . . He was further surprised to learn that Juanita Barbee, Roosevelt's secretary, is a friend of Wilkinson's ..." [57]

Cooperation with the FBI was the rule rather than the exception for individuals, groups and agencies, private and governmental. This willingness to help the FBI, regardless of the invasion of privacy and constitutional rights, coupled with the assumption that the FBI could do no wrong, invested the Bureau with awesome power and multiplied its resources. In the late fifties, this cooperation stretched across the political spectrum from the American Legion to the American Civil Liberties Union*, and across occupational lines from local police departments to landlords, neighbors, bank managers and university presidents. In some cases, assistance in the FBI's heresy hunting was motivated by the belief that this was the price of staying off the FBI's subversive list.

The American Legion

The American Legion was undoubtedly the FBI's most important non-governmental accomplice, thanks to the Legion's political influence as the major veterans' organization in the country. The common ideology shared by J. Edgar Hoover and the Legion leadership made it a durable relationship with little need for concealment. Through the machinery of the network of Americanism Committees, headed by Hoover's aide, Cartha DeLoach*, communications were effective down to the local level through FBI Field Offices. A cadre of ideologically motivated members were on call for immediate mobilization. Legionnaires often volunteered their services as informers, like ▓▓▓▓▓ ▓▓▓▓▓▓▓▓▓▓ in Cincinnati, who wrote the NCAHUAC national and regional offices, pretending to be a person opposed to HUAC seeking the names of contacts in the area. When the national office volunteer trustingly sent him its list in Cincinnati, it was turned over to the FBI Field Office. The FBI promptly identified and indexed a group in which it found "identifiable subversive derogatory" characteristics, such as "writing letters to the editor," "activity in the ACLU," or engaging in "activities of a controversial nature such as doing away with the death penalty."[59]

The Legion was the FBI's shock troop for the disruption of meetings. Legionnaires, like John Bollenbeck, a retired Army officer and chair of the Madison, Wis. Americanism Committee, could be counted on to attend meetings opposing HUAC and to ask hostile questions from the floor.

On May 7, 1963, a meeting in Evanston, Ill. was violently disrupted by a group led by men in Le-

* DeLoach ran the FBI operation so smoothly that by the early 1960s, Hoover's close friend Walter Trohan, Washington Bureau chief of the Chicago Tribune was struck by the totality of the Bureau's domination. In a letter to Hoover, Trohan wrote: "It was a most refreshing experience for me to attend the American Legion Convention, and find people cheering the country and its traditions and saluting the flag instead of cheering the ADA [Americans for Democratic Action] and calling for conciliation of Communists . . . It was also an invaluable experience, because I find the American Legion is an adjunct of the FBI with FBI men writing speeches for prominent orators, drafting resolutions and sparking the show generally." [58]

gion caps. The speakers, Frank Wilkinson and Rev. Wyatt Tee Walker, an aide of the Rev. Martin Luther King, Jr., were booed so loudly that they could not be heard. The meeting was jointly sponsored by eleven Evanston groups, including the NAACP, the American Jewish Congress, a number of churches and the Human Relations Council, but this made it no less subversive in the minds of the attackers. The organizer of the meeting had to swear out arrest warrants and demand that the police remove the disrupters to finally restore order.[60]

In Banks We Dare Not Trust

Bank customers assume their financial records are confidential and private. Officially, the bank will not show such documents to anyone unless ordered to do so by a subpoena *duces tecum*. In reality the banks have followed, covertly, a quite different policy. Significantly, the first item in the National Committee to Abolish HUAC file is a directive to the Los Angeles Field Office: "...at the first indication that captioned organization has set up a bank account, you should set up procedures to monitor this account and incorporate the data received in an organizational report."[61]

The above directive was an FBI Standing Operating Procedure with which all banks apparently cooperated. The covert agreement required that the spied upon bank customer be denied the information that his account was secretly monitored by the FBI.* Every group cooperating with the National Committee to Abolish HUAC had its bank account regularly monitored, in Chicago, New York, Los Angeles, Milwaukee, San Francisco, Boston and elsewhere. Each Field Office included this financial data in its regular reports to National

* *"It is believed that in order to more appropriately conceal the fact that we obtain information from bank records that such specific references should not be utilized in the future."—Director to SAC, Los Angeles[62]*

Headquarters. The private accounts of leadership individuals were also perused. Each person who wrote a check payable to any of these groups was routinely "indexed" by the Bureau. Thus the FBI knew financial problems and the names of major contributors; with this "intelligence," the Bureau knew where to direct its *neutralization* projects to inflict maximum damage on the organization. When the FBI learned of large contributions from unknown donors, it went to extraordinary lengths, including burglaries, to find the identity of the "UNSUB"—unknown subject.*

Red Squads

Along with the American Legion and the banks, the most important elements in the FBI's cooperative network were the local police, especially their "anti-subversive details" or "Red Squads". The "Red Squad" was usually a section of the major city police "intelligence division" which modeled its operations on the FBI's "internal security" i.e. non-criminal work. They often conducted surveillance on the same targets as the FBI, and recruited their own small armies of infiltrators.

Indicative of the close working relationship was a wire from the Los Angeles Field Office to the Director informing him of an assassination plot against Frank Wilkinson. The act was scheduled to be carried out on March 4, 1964 while Wilkinson was addressing an ACLU meeting in a private home. The FBI's confidential source for this information was the head of the Los Angeles Police Anti-Subversive Detail. Whatever police action was contemplated was left to the LAPD, which planned a stakeout at the site of the projected assassination. The following day the Field Office was informed that no attempt on Wilkinson's life had

* For example, the office of the Chicago Committee to Defend the Bill of Rights was twice burglarized to identify "UNSUBS" on Feb. 2, 1962 and Jan. 10, 1966, in two different office locations. Each burglary was authorized in a special memo by an assistant director of the FBI and the SAC [Special Agent in Charge] of the Chicago Field Office, marked "NOT FOR FILE." Both memos noted the landlords were cooperative, though not necessarily informed of the FBI's intended felony.

taken place. No further reference occurs in the files and apparently no FBI follow-up action was contemplated. No steps were taken by either the LAPD or the FBI to inform Wilkinson of the assassination plot. As the FBI memo notes:

Wilkinson identified as Communist Party member in past and in recent years associated with communist-dominated groups such as Citizens Committee to Preserve American Freedoms and National Committee to Abolish House Un-American Activities Committee, devoted to abolishing the House Committee on Un-American Activities.

Evidently, in a case where the intended victim had such subversive credentials, the FBI had little interest in protecting his life.[63]

Not only did the Red Squads provide additional eyes and ears for the FBI, but they conducted *neutralization* projects either in conjunction with the FBI or independently against the same targets. Lawsuits against the Red Squads in Chicago and Los Angeles revealed an extraordinary degree of collaboration between the federal and local agencies, virtually merging their political surveillance and neutralization efforts. With its greater resources, prestige, experience and political sophistication, the Federal Bureau was the leader and mentor. A rough division of labor occurred, where the Red Squad in Chicago, secure in the protections of the political patronage machine, was more willing to engage in flagrant violations of the law. In studying the records of *neutralization* operations, it is often impossible to find out where the FBI connection left off and where the local political police took over. Wholesale destruction of documents* means that we may never learn the full details.

* In the Chicago lawsuit, Alliance to End Repression v. City of Chicago, which began against the Red Squad, and was enlarged to encompass the FBI, the Chicago police informer who was privy to reports of Alliance legal strategies, reported that the lawsuit was about to be filed. A massive burning of Red Squad documents followed, until stopped by order of the federal court. It is a reasonable assumption that the bulk of the incriminating documents were destroyed. A similar destruction of Red Squad documents occurred in Memphis. In 1975, the ACLU of Tennessee filed a suit against the Memphis Police Dept. for their spying on Mike Honey, then-director of NCARL's Southern Regional Office. Immediately, after the legal action was filed, the Memphis police burned the records sought.

How The FBI Used Informer Testimony

While our narrative has dealt with the FBI's copious use of undercover infiltrators in its *neutralization* operations, it is instructive to examine in detail the use of testimony of one such informer.

On 12/7/56, Anita Edith Bell Schneider, FBI San Diego informant, SD 851-S, testified before the House Un-American Activities Committee that she knew Frank Wilkinson to have been a member of the Communist Party some time between 1951 and 1956.

This testimony was a key element in the initial conviction of Wilkinson in Atlanta in January 1959 and in the Supreme Court's decision on 2/27/61 to uphold his conviction for contempt of Congress.[64]

Following the public announcement of the formation of the National Committee to Abolish HUAC, Schneider's testimony was included in the "public source" material provided Fulton Lewis, Jr. for his article of 10/27/60 in the New York "Daily Mirror":

> Wilkenson (sic) is only one of seven identified Communists on the 15-man national committee. Identified under oath by FBI undercover agent Anita Schneider in 1956..."

Cartha DeLoach provided this material to his media contacts for use in stories intended to denigrate the National Committee.

Despite its reliance upon Schneider's HUAC testimony, the Bureau had been aware, even *prior to her appearance as a HUAC witness in 1956*, that she was untrustworthy and unbelievable. A Los Angeles memo notes the "information regarding Wilkinson's CP membership comes from sources not considered advisable to use as government witnesses."*

* On February 23, 1989, lawyers for Frank Wilkinson filed a coram Nobis petition with the U.S. District Court for the Northern District of Georgia, claiming that the conviction was based on government misconduct involving the use of an unreliable witness.

The memo records:

The Bureau, by letter dated 11/7/61, to Los Angeles in another matter, instructed that in view of the background of **Anita Edith Schneider** it is not believed advisable to make her identity available to the Department of Defense in connection with that matter. San Diego, by letter dated 10/17/61 to the Bureau, stated that **Schneider** testified before the Subversive Activities Control Board in March, 1955, at which time she exhibited emotional instability and that since 1955, pursuant to Bureau instructions, no further contact has been had with **Schneider**, and her present whereabouts are unknown to the San Diego office.[65]

The Bureau's knowledge that the testimony was probably perjured did not inhibit its use for the next seven years.

Why Was The National Committee Able To Survive?

By 1965, it was already clear that the momentum was on the side of the opponents of HUAC. The Chicago HUAC hearing that spring resulted in a serious political defeat for the House Committee; it would never again hold a hearing outside of the protective walls of the nation's capital. More than four years of J. Edgar Hoover's clandestine war against the National Committee had failed to deliver a knockout blow, or stop its growth. Hoover was used to winning battles against his chosen enemies. Why weren't his weapons inflicting mortal wounds? Why did the apparently frail National Committee stay in the ring, when others were left hanging on the ropes? The strategy of *neutralization* was to isolate a group from its public base of support. As our narrative suggests, although it won some battles, the FBI lost the war.

The first asset of the National Committee was the quality of its leadership. The initial trio of Alexander Meiklejohn, Aubrey Williams and Frank Wilkinson attracted the support and commitment of an unusual and diverse group: James Imbrie, a retired New Jersey banker; Professor H.H.Wilson of Princeton University, who was the first academic to challenge J. Edgar Hoover head on; Professor Otto Nathan, the German-born anti-fascist executor of Albert Einstein's estate; Clarence Pickett, Director Emeritus of the American Friends Service Committee; University of Chicago Professor Robert J. Havighurst, a former student of Meiklejohn, and a leading figure in the world of education; Harvey O'Connor, the muckraking author who defied Senator Joe McCarthy and got away with it; veteran union leader, Russ Nixon; Sylvia Crane, historian, fund-raiser and organizer; the Reverend William T. Baird and Richard Criley, who organized the committee's midwest base in Chicago; White integrationists Carl and Anne Braden; the Reverend C.T. Vivian, of the Southern Christian Leadership conference; John Lewis*, past chair of the militant Student Non-Violent Coordinating Committee (SNCC); Professor Thomas I. Emerson of Yale Law School and the recognized top legal scholar on the First Amendment; Professor Vern Countryman of Harvard Law School; Dr. Donna Allen, the National Committee's first Washington Representative; Dorothy Marshall, past president of the Catholic Women's Club of Los Angeles; and others too numerous to mention.

Currently a U.S. Representative from Atlanta, Ga.

This leadership was able to rally allies like Eleanor Roosevelt, who spoke out publicly against the House Committee. Against such well known public figures, HUAC's counterattacks based on guilt by association were not convincing, and ended in making its "subversive lists" look like an honor roll.

The amnesty petitions for Braden and Wilkinson had received over three thousand endorsements from leaders of the academic, religious and professional communities. In early 1964, the National Committee sent letters to a selected group soliciting their support as sponsors for the committee. The letter warned prospective sponsors that they might suffer retaliation from HUAC if they lent their names. The warning did not reduce the number of favorable responses. The National Committee had to devise a special four-page letterhead to list the more than four hundred who put their names on the line. By the mid sixties, the intellectual elite of the country had taken a stand in opposition to HUAC. As the National Committee intensified work on a Congressional District level, petitions were signed by hundreds of local "opinion makers." These were key to winning support from Representatives to cut HUAC appropriations and vote for its abolition.

As our history indicates, college students played a major role in challenging HUAC . The battle was joined after the San Francisco 1960 hearing when "Operation Abolition" was shown at hundreds of campuses, and the resulting debate caused students to choose sides. While a right-wing minority organized the pro-HUAC "Young Americans for Freedom," far larger numbers were joining the struggle to abolish it. The generally hostile atmosphere on campus caused the FBI to tiptoe around operations which could trigger cries of violation of academic freedom. The Chicago Field Office excused its 1962 failure to develop disruptive operations against a student anti-HUAC conference: "This is very unfavorable grounds for any counter-intelligence measure since the atmosphere among University of Chicago students is not conducive to any adult censure without absolute documentation of the [subversive] nature of MSCLCC [the Midwest Student Civil Liberties Coordinating Committee]"[66]

As students were breaking out of the bonds of Cold War ideology, the Black freedom movement arose to challenge it on another front. Black leaders were learning through bitter experience that red-baiting was a standard weapon of southern segregationists to discourage white support for integration. When HUAC scheduled its hearings in Atlanta in 1958, leading to the prison sentences of Braden and Wilkinson, all but one of the subpoenaed civil rights activists were white. Two hundred and ten Southern civil rights leaders signed a petition to Congress asking that the House Committee stay out of the South. To consolidate its alliance with the civil rights movement, the National Committee published a pamphlet by Anne Braden, "HUAC, Bulwark of Segregation," and undertook to distribute two-hundred thousand copies.

When the FBI's informers reported on this projected publication, the Bureau worked frantically to obtain an advance copy of the text, so that the Crime Records Division could negate its impact. When Headquarters finally received copies from Los Angeles, the staff memo records with some relief that, "There is no reference to the FBI or the Director in the pamphlet."[67] In any case, the FBI failed to thwart distribution of the pamphlet, and the educational message it contained strengthened grassroots alliances with civil rights activists.

HUAC Makes Tactical Retreats

As HUAC lost support in the general population, the opposition mounted in the House of Representatives. HUAC was compelled to make a number of tactical retreats, which diminished its effectiveness. By foregoing its hearings across the country, to avoid the growing numbers of protesters, it lost its ability to command headlines in the local news media. Added to the increased level of resistance from unfriendly witnesses were Supreme Court decisions in 1969 and 1972 which outlawed electronic surveillance without warrants and permitted defense attorneys to examine wiretap records. These made it difficult and inexpedient to prosecute recalcitrant witnesses for contempt of Congress.[68] The House Committee was also put on the defensive by law suits filed by three Chicago 1965 hearing witnesses, Dr. Jeremiah Stamler, Yolanda Hall and Milton Cohen.

With the rise of the civil rights and anti-war movements, dissent in America assumed a mass character with new protagonists who could not be linked to the Communist Party. HUAC's old stock-in-trade of red-baiting and guilt-by-association with the "old left" became obsolete. The FBI remodelled its *neutralization* techniques so as to function without reliance on HUAC—a change symbolized by the new caption: COINTELPRO—NEW LEFT.

The challenges of these new mass movements gave the FBI a more pressing priority than the *neutralization* of the National Committee to Abolish HUAC.

HUAC endured, under a different name, the House Internal Security Committee, and with a lowered profile, until the exposures of the Watergate era. By then, even the FBI faced meaningful restrictions on its power to conduct political surveillance and *neutralization.* In 1975, HUAC/HISC passed away in a reorganization of House Committees.

Reform of the FBI was imposed from outside. To forestall more binding legislative regulations, Attorney General Edward H. Levi issued a set of guidelines implicitly prohibiting *neutralization* and political surveillance in domestic security cases. The appointment of former federal judge William Webster to head the FBI seemed end the FBI violations of constitutional rights. But did it?

The State of Mind Within the Bureau

The state of mind of the senior FBI agents who had been trained and practiced under the tutelage of J. Edgar Hoover was not so easily changed by guidelines and a change of top command.

The closeout document in the NCARL file, from the Los Angeles Field Office to the Director, dated 4/14/75 carries the following "predicate":

> National Committee Against Repressive Legislation (NCARL)
>
> Internal Security—Communist Party, USA
>
> Internal Security Act of 1950
>
> This investigation is based on information which indicates that the National Committee Against Repressive Legislation (NCARL) is engaged in activities which could involve a violation of Title 18, United States Code, Section 2383 (Rebellion or Insurrection), 2384 (Seditious Conspiracy), 2385 (Advocating Overthrow of the Government), or Title 50, United States Code, Sections 781 -798 (Internal Security Act of 1950).

The report, remarkably brief when compared to the 60-page productions which were issued regularly during the preceding fifteen years, reads in its essential statements:

> (redacted) Frank Byron Wilkinson continues as the Executive Director and Field Representative of NCARL. Source characterized the NCARL as being primarily a mailing list maintained by Wilkinson

rather than a membership group. Wilkinson, assisted by volunteers, makes massive mailings of literature calling for action against repressive legislation. Wilkinson also makes some speeches to various groups around the country promoting action against repressive legislation, primarily in the form of urging writing to one's Congressman or Senator...

The report's appendix quotes the "Guide to Subversive Organizations and Publications," issued 12/1/61 by HUAC to the effect that:
"Cited as a 'new organization' set up in the summer of 1960, to lead and direct the Communist Party's 'Operation Abolition' campaign. Seven of the national leaders of this group have been identified as communists."

The cover page to the LHM (Letterhead Memo) states:
No further information has come to light in Los Angeles regarding a possible suit by **Frank Byron Wilkinson** under the Freedom of Information Act.

In view of the fact that there is no ongoing investigation required in this matter, this case is being closed in Los Angeles. If pertinent information is developed, the Bureau will be advised.[69]

Thus we observe that it took fifteen years for the most sophisticated and heavily funded police investigative organization in the world to determine that NCARL was not engaged in Rebellion or Insurrection, Seditious Conspiracy, Advocating Overthrow of the Government, or failure to register as an organization controlled and dominated by the Communist Party, USA.

During those fifteen years, an unknown number of paid undercover informers reported to their Special Agent case officers, who generated over 130,000 pages of reports at a cost of several million dollars. For most of those years a special corps of agents, in deepest secrecy, conducted an illegal conspiracy under color of law to deprive NCARL participants of their civil liberties, and the American people of their constitutional right to be informed about HUAC and repressive legislation.

Many of the agents who perpetrated these offenses and illegally harassed their fellow citizens in the belief that this was their patriotic duty are still working for and leading the Federal Bureau of Investigation. Recent events suggest that the state-of-mind which produced the attempted *neutralization* of NCARL has not changed.

Afterword

What can be done to prevent the reemergence of the constitutional violations described in the NCARL story? Current exposures indicate that they can and do recur. *Parade Magazine*, a supplement to Sunday newspapers across the country, devoted a major story to this problem. It carried the following statement regarding current FBI Director William Sessions' prospects:

Sessions' honor, integrity and good intentions were not at issue. The question most often raised was whether he—or anyone—would be able to control the FBI or whether its fabled bureaucracy has spun an unbreakable web around him.[70]

Professor Athan Theoharis concludes his definitive biography of J. Edgar Hoover with the question: "Did Hoover's death end the possibility, or at least the likelihood, of FBI abuse?" After describing the post-Watergate reform measures, and the rescinding of those regulations under the Reagan Administration, he concludes:

In the final analysis, then, Congress' failure to enact an FBI legislative charter left the way open for another director-adventurer who, by exploiting a crisis atmosphere and supported by conservative anti-Communists, could reinstitute yet another reactionary scare and a wholesale repression. The potential for abuse did not die with Hoover in 1972.[71]

Appendix

Preface to Judge A. Wallace Tashima's Memorandum Decision and Order of January 9, 1990

Publication of the educational pamphlet you have just read was delayed by nearly four months because of a claim by the United States Department of Justice that Frank Wilkinson and the National Committee Against Repressive Legislation had voluntarily agreed not to publicly disclose or otherwise "use" any of the information provided to them after 1984 in their lawsuit against the Federal Bureau of Investigation. *See Frank Wilkinson, et al. v. Federal Bureau of Investigation, et al.*, United States District Court, Central District of California, Case No. CV 80-1048 AWT (Tx).

In September of 1989, pursuant to a pre-trial "protective order" entered in the *Wilkinson* case, plaintiffs' attorneys presented the Justice Department's lawyers with a draft of this pamphlet and requested that they permit its immediate publication. The Justice Department refused, stating without further explanation that the protective order's supposed "use" restriction "is very important to the FBI." The Department even declined to participate in negotiations intended to resolve its concerns, declaring it did "not believe that further discussions would be fruitful."

Consequently, plaintiffs' attorneys prepared a

motion seeking a court order to permit the publication of this pamphlet over the federal government's objection. That motion was heard in Los Angeles by United States District Court Judge A. Wallace Tashima on December 18, 1989. Three weeks later, Judge Tashima issued a written opinion authorizing publication of the pamphlet you have just read and permitting public disclosure of various underlying documents from the FBI's files. Characterizing the Justice Department's tortured interpretation of the 1984 protective order in this case as "nonsensical," Judge Tashima's opinion adopts plaintiffs' view that, under this order, "disclosure may be made of any document which does not reveal the identity of any non-public figure person." The complete text of Judge Tashima's January 9, 1990, opinion is reprinted below:

United States District Court
Central District of California
Frank Wilkinson, et al. Plaintiffs, v. Federal Bureau of Investigation, et al., Defendants.

"No. CV 80-1048 AWT Memorandum Decision and Order

"This ten-year old action, involving events which occurred 30-40 years ago, is once again before the Court, this time for resolution of a dispute involving the meaning of a stipulation and order made six years ago.

"For those of us old enough to remember, it was a tumultuous time in our nation's recent history. With hindsight and in the aura of glasnost, some would easily call it an unfortunate period. **Plaintiff Frank Wilkinson was a well-known participant in certain of the political events of that era. He, and others, instituted this action to right the wrongs the FBI committed upon him at that time. The public record discloses that the FBI's actions with respect to him and the**

Boldface type denotes emphasis added here.

organizations with which he was affiliated were less than exemplary. It would serve no purpose to detail those actions here. Plaintiff received no monetary compensation in this action, but during its course, through either Freedom of Information Act, 5 U.S.C. 552 (FOIA), requests and orders to enforce them or through discovery, plaintiff did receive a substantial volume of FBI documents concerning its surveillance and investigation of his activities.

"Plaintiff now wishes to publish a pamphlet on this subject. The pamphlet necessarily discloses information gained through discovery in this action.* Plaintiff believes he is entitled to disclose this information gained from the FBI. The FBI disagrees. If not so entitled, plaintiff seeks modification of the protective order to permit him to do so. This part of the motion also is opposed by the FBI.

"On November 30, 1984, a Second Stipulation Re Discovery; Order Thereon, was entered in this action. The relevant portions of that stipulation and order provide:

"*(5) It is agreed by plaintiffs and defendants that all documents and things which the FBI produces pursuant to paragraph 1 of the First Stipulation shall not be redacted to delete the names or other identifying characteristics of third persons based upon such persons interest in personal privacy, provided that access to all such documents is limited to the parties in this action, their counsel, and to such other persons to whom disclosure of such documents may reasonably be necessary for the preparation of motions in this case, or use as evidence or exhibits in deposition,** and for trial preparation by counsel, their staffs and experts, and witnesses in this case. As used herein, the term third persons refers to all persons and entities other than the named plaintiffs, the defendants then before the*

*The pamphlet, in part, details the FBI's actions and inactions with respect to plaintiff which were unknown to him. For example, at one point, the FBI was furnished with credible information that an assassination attempt would be made on Wilkinson. Although observers were sent to the scene to see what might happen, no attempt was made to warn Wilkinson. Fortunately, the attempt never took place.

**In the event a document is used as an exhibit in pretrial depositions, the exhibit and the testimony relating to it shall remain subject to the provisions of the Stipulation and Order. That is, disclosure beyond the parties, their attorneys and their experts and assistants does not become authorized merely by use of a document in a deposition.

It is understood that the FBI's files may contain unverified information relating to third parties disclosure of which to anyone would be an unwarranted invasion of privacy. An example of such information would be an allegation that a named judge accepted bribes. In such a case the FBI may delete the name of the person or other identifying information, coding the deletion with deletion code "O."

Court and the individuals identified in paragraph 2 of the Stipulation.*

"6) In the event that the plaintiffs or their attorneys wish to disclose publicly any of the documents produced by the FBI which contain the names or other identifying characteristics of third persons, they shall first obtain and transmit to counsel for the FBI a privacy waiver verified as provided in 28 U.S.C. Sec. 1746, from the person or persons involved. In the event such a waiver cannot be secured, counsel for the plaintiffs will confer with counsel for the FBI in an attempt to secure their concurrence in public disclosure of the document. Such concurrence shall be memorialized by Stipulation, and no public release may be made until that stipulation is approved by the Court. In the event that agreement cannot be reached, the plaintiffs may seek leave of Court to disclose to the public the document or documents in question. Nothing in this paragraph is intended to nor does it in fact limit any disclosure of documents or things admitted as evidence at the trial, or at any pretrial evidentiary hearing, in this action.

"(7) Nothing in paragraph 5 or 6 of the Stipulation and Order shall in any way limit the right of the plaintiffs or their counsel to publicly disclose any document which reveals only the identities of public figures. As used herein, 'public figures' includes all elected officials of federal, State or municipal government; all judges, whether or not elected; and appointed officials of the United States who hold an office appointment to which is made by the President with the advice and consent of the Senate, whether or not the incumbent of the office identified in the document is regularly appointed or serving by virtue of a recess appointment or in an acting capacity. With respect to all other persons whom the plaintiffs may deem to be public figures, plaintiffs' *and the FBI's counsel have agreed to confer in an attempt to reach an agreement on the 'public figure' status of the individual(s) involved. If the agreement cannot be reached, or if a verified privacy waiver(s) cannot be secured, the plaintiffs may apply to the Court for leave to release the document to the public.*

"The stipulation is something of a 'hybrid.' While it was intended to govern discovery, it also was in partial settlement of plaintiff's claims under FOIA.

"Because, for the reason stated below, the Court concludes that the disclosures plaintiff seeks to make are authorized by the stipulation, it does not reach the issues of whether or not the stipulation should be modified or whether First Amendment issues are implicated.

"Although the stipulation was approved by and entered as an order of the Court, it is essentially an agreement between the parties and should be construed as such. The purposes to be accomplished by paragraph (5) are evident on its face: Plaintiff would obtain unredacted documents, but information which defendant would otherwise be entitled to redact would not be disclosed.* There appears to be no legitimate purpose of the FBI to be served by paragraph (5), except to protect the privacy interest of persons whose identities would be disclosed under its provisions.** There is no legitimate interest in preventing public disclosure of discovery documents in this action, once privacy information which would otherwise have been redacted is deleted.

"Moreover, paragraph (7) plainly overrides paragraph (5). It permits the disclosure of 'any document which reveals only the identities of public figures.' **Defendant construes this, nonsensically, as referring only to documents consisting entirely of the identities of public figures, i.e.,**

*The FBI contends that the Court has already determined the scope of paragraph (5) by its order of April 4, 1989. However, that order specifically concerned the privacy interest of a non-public figure person and there was no occasion to discuss the relationship between paragraphs (5) and (7).

**While contending that the stipulation's "use" restriction is "important" to the FBI, no reason is given for that claimed importance. When questioned at oral argument as to the FBI's interest in opposing plaintiff's motion, aside from the privacy issue, counsel's only response, in substance, was the FBI's interest in requiring plaintiff to live up to his agreement.

Boldface type denotes emphasis added here.

a list of public figures. Of course, there is no such list. More sensibly, the Court interprets this to mean that disclosure may be made of any document which does not reveal the identity of any non-public figure person.

"Paragraph (6) provides that, ultimately, the Court may authorize disclosure of documents which identify third persons.* This authority, apparently, is independent of Paragraph (7), i.e., whether or not the persons involved are public figures. No detailed analysis of this paragraph need be made, however, because the plaintiff does not intend to disclose the identity of any non-public figure.

*It is because of this authority that the motion for modification is mooted. This also means that disclosure is consistent with defendant's insistence that plaintiff be required to live up to his bargain. Part of that bargain is the Court's retained authority to authorize disclosure.

"Moreover, in his reply, plaintiff has agreed to accept defendant's inchoate 'compromise' offer, as set forth in footnote 10, p.24, of the Rule 7.15.2 Joint Stipulation. That note states:

"*For example, plaintiffs present no explanation for their apparent conclusion that their goals would not be wholly satisfied by using general descriptions in place of names received from discovery in this case, e.g., 'a candidate for public office in Canada,' or 'the police force in a major city' or 'a staff member of HUAC.'*

"The Court accepts plaintiff's offer, as it moots the need for the Court to determine whether two individuals whose identities plaintiff desires to disclose are (today) public figures. However, the Court believes that the public figure doctrine does not apply to governmental agencies. Government, by definition, cannot ever be a private person. It has no privacy interest, constitutional or otherwise. No public interest is served by not fully disclosing the actions of government, absent of a legitimate and articulable reason for secrecy. Thus, the Court rules that nothing in the second stipulation prevents the disclosure of the identity of the 'Metropolitan Police Department of Washington, D.C.'

"IT IS ORDERED:

"1. Plaintiff's request for 'enforcement' of protective order is granted in part.

"2. Plaintiff may publicly disclose those documents, copies of which are appended as Exhibit 'C' to the declaration of Douglas E. Mirell, filed under seal on or about December 4, 1989.

"3. Plaintiff may not publicly disclose the identities of the two individuals who are identified by name in the draft 'The FBI vs. The First Amendment,' appended as Exhibit 'A' to the Mirell declaration, and whose status as public figures is disputed by the parties. Said individuals shall be referred to only as 'a candidate for public office in Canada' and 'a staff member of HUAC,' or by similar descriptive phrases.

"4. Public figure versus non-public figure status does not apply to the government or its agencies. No identifiable privacy interest of a governmental agency has been shown. Thus, the second stipulation's public figure limitation does not apply to the 'Metropolitan Police Department of Washington, D.C.'

"Dated: January, 09, 1990

"A. Wallace Tashima
"United States District Judge"

Endnotes

1. Kenneth O'Reilly, p. 291, "Hoover and the Un-Americans," Temple University Press, Philadelphia 1983

2. Ross Gelbspan, Boston Globe, 7/24/88.

3. CISPES file, 199-5848-128x, SECRET declassified 7/17/87.

4. Gelbspan, Boston Globe, 3/15/88; also Center for Constitutional Rights, "Selected Headquarters CISPES documents," document 10, dated 7/12/84.

5. Gelbspan, Boston Globe, 1/27/88.

6. Testimony before the House Judiciary Subcommittee on Civil and Constitutional Rights, 9/14-16/88, quoted in The Right to Know and Freedom to Act, July, 1988.

7. The Right to Know and Freedom to Act, July, 1988.

8. Anne Braden, "The FBI vs. Black Voting Rights, A Case Study of Racial Harassment," NCARL brochure.

9. Philip Shenon, The New York Times, 7/4/88.

10. Associated Press dispatch, The Herald, Monterey, CA, 11/1/88.

11. HQS (Richard Criley) 100-26576-11; also O'Reilly, p. 317 ibid.

12. House Judiciary Subcommittee on Civil and Constitutional Rights, Oversight Hearings, part I, First Session, 1977.

13. HQS (NCARL) 100-433447, Sub A not registered dated 10/9/60 and nos 23 & 28.

14. HQS 100-433447-1,2,8,11,14, NR 10/7/60.

15. Time Magazine, Education section, 11/19/60.

16. HQS (Frank Wilkinson) 100-112434-1.

17. O'Reilly, p. 207, ibid.

18. HQS 100-112434-17.

19. HQS 100-112434 NR 5/4/53.

20. Los Angeles (Frank Wilkinson) 100-16439-713.

21. LA 100-16439-2509.

22. LA 100-16439-2042.

23. LA 100-16439-714 and 2043.

24. HQS 100-433447-36 to 76.

25. HQS 100-112434-83.

26. Reporter magazine, 11/24/60.

27. NY (NCARL) 100-142201-36; HQS 100-433447-40.

28. HQS 100-433447-50. NR teletype 12/30/60.

29. HQS 100-433447-57.

30. HQS 100-433447-81; COINTEL 104-3-10-2233 p. 6

31. HQS 100-433447-49-56-78.

32. HQS 100-433447-71.

33. Washington Field Office (WF)) (NCARL) 100-37885-77.

34. HQS 100-112434-107.

35. HQS 100-112434-114.

36. HQS 100-112434-122.

37. Philadelphia (Frank Wilkinson) 100- 44603-15 and 20; HQS 100-112434- NR 1/24/61 and NR 1/30/62.

38. HQS 100-112434-107.

39. HQS 100-433447-166x.

40. HQS 100-112434—not registered dated 11/8/61.

41. HQS 100-112434—not registered dated 4/19/62.

42. HQS 100-433447-196.

43. HQS COINTELPRO 100-3-104-43-24, 47x; 100-3-104-34-280.

44. HQS 100-433447-198.

45. HQS 100-433447-199; Chicago COINTELPRO 100-32864-1166, 1228.

46. HQS COINTELPRO 100-3-104-280;100-3-104-11-22,25,30.

47. HQS COINTELPRO 100-3-104-34-280.

48. HQS COINTELPRO 100-3-104-9-80.

49. HQS COINTELPRO 100-3-104-47; Minneapolis (NCARL) 100-12627-424.

50. HQS COINTELPRO 100-3-104-52-4.

51. HQS COINTELPRO 100-3-104-4739; HQS 100-433447— not registered dated 10/21/63.

52. HQS 100-433447—not registered dated 11/15/63.

53. HQS 100-433447-500.

54. O'Reilly, p.280, ibid.

55.HQS 100-433447-727

56. HQS 100-433447 not registered 6/12/70 (COINTELPRO NEW LEFT)

57. HQS 100-112434 not registered dated 7/29/58.

58. O'Reilly, p.89, ibid.

59. HQS 100-433447-305.

60. Chicago 100-36797, vol. 3; Chicago (NCARL) 100-37438 -50.

61. HQS 100-433447-1.

62. HQS 100-433447-44b.

63. HQS 100-112434-164, 165.

64. 365 US 399 Frank Wilkinson v. the United States, paras. 365,406,413,418,419.

65. Los Angeles 100-16439-2509 dated 11/21/61.

66. Chicago 100-32864-1175.

67. HQS 100-433447-412, 477.

68. O'Reilly, p. 284 ibid.

69. HQS 100-433447-797.

70. Peter Mass, Parade Magazine, 12/18/88.

71. Athan Theoharis and John Stuart Cox, "The Boss," p. 435, Temple University Press, Philadelphia, 1988.

First Amendment Foundation

1313 West 8th Street, Suite 313, Los Angeles, California 90017
Approved, Internal Revenue Service, Federal Income Tax Exemption,
Sec. 501(c)(3), I.D. 95-3922815

Board of Directors:

Chauncey A. Alexander, President

Professor, Lecturer, California State University, Long Beach, Department of Social Work.
Executive Director, National Association of Social Workers, 1969-82. President and Treasurer, International Federation of Social Workers, 1976-82. Board Chair, Council on Hemispheric Affairs, 1976-82. Associate Director, Regional Medical Programs, UCLA School of Medicine, and Senior Lecturer, UCLA Schools of Public Health and Social Welfare, 1967-69. Executive Director, Los Angeles County Heart Association, 1956-67. Program Director, LACHA, 1954-56. Executive Director, Southern California Society for Mental Hygiene. Research and Public Information Director, Los Angeles Veterans Service Center. OTHER: Recipient: National Association of Social Workers' "Lifetime Achievement Award," California "Koshland Award," Orange County's "Human Relations Award." AUTHOR: "International Policy on Human Rights and International Code of Ethics for Social Workers" for IFSW; "China View"; "Professional Liability: Jeopardy and Ethics"; "Professional Social Workers and Political Responsibility"; "Management in Human Service Organizations"; et al.

Carole Goldberg Ambrose, Secretary

Professor of Law, UCLA School of Law; Associate Dean, 1984-89. Law Clerk to Honorable Robert F. Peckham, 1971-72. Visiting Professor of Law, Harvard Law School. AUTHOR: "Handbook of Federal Indian Law"; "The Protective Jurisdiction of the Federal Courts" UCLA Law Review; "The Influence of Procedural Rules on Federal Jurisdiction" Stanford Law Review; "Issues of Special Concern to Women," Looking at Law Schools; "S. 1437 is a Legal Nightmare" The Judges Journal, American Bar Association; "Closing the Federal Courthouse to Public Interest Litigations" U.S. Senate Judiciary Committee; et al.

Vern Countryman

Professor Emeritus, Harvard Law School.
Dean, University of New Mexico Law School, 1955-64. Associate Professor, Yale Law School, 1948-55. Clerk to Mr. Justice William O. Douglas, 1942-43. President, Clerks of Mr. Justice William O. Douglas. AUTHOR: "Debtors' and Creditors' Rights"; "Un-American Activities in the State of Washington"; "The States and Subversion"; "Douglas of the Supreme Court"; "The Lawyer in Modern Society"; "Discrimination and the Law"; "Featherbedding and Technological Change"; "Commercial Law"; "The Judicial Record of Justice William O. Douglas"; et al.

Irving Dilliard

Author, Educator, Editor.
Member Incorporator, National News Council, 1973-1977. Director, Illinois Department of Aging, 1974-75. Ferris Professor of Journalism, Princeton University, 1963-73. Distinguished Lecturer, Universities of: Illinois; Colby College; Brandeis; New Mexico; Oregon; Depauw; Kansas; Nevada; Salzburg; California 1949-63. Correspon-

dent, Editorial Writer, Editor, Editorial Page, St. Louis Post-Dispatch, 1923-60. AUTHOR: "Building the Constitution"; "The Development of Free Press in Germany"; "I'm From Missouri"; Editor, "Mr. Justice Brandeis, Great American"; "The Spirit of Liberty"; "Papers and Addresses of Leonard Hand"; "One Man's Stand for Freedom: Mr. Justice Black and the Bill of Rights"; et al.

Thomas I. Emerson

Professor Emeritus, Yale Law School.
General Counsel, Office of War Mobilization and Reconversion. General Counsel, Office of Economic Stabilization. Associate General Counsel and Deputy Administrator, OPA. Special Assistant to Attorney General, Department of Justice. Principal Attorney, Social Security Board. Associate General Counsel, NLRB. OTHER: Visiting Professor, London School of Economics & Brookings Institution; Guggenheim Fellow; Fulbright Fellow; Member & former President, National Lawyers Guild. AUTHOR: "Political and Civil Rights in the United States"; "Toward a General Theory of the First Amendment"; "The System of Freedom of Expression"; et al.

Fred J. Gianola

Clinical Investigator, Fred Hutchinson Cancer Research Center, Seattle, Washington.
Clinical Investigator, National Cancer Institute, Bethesda, Maryland. Physician Assistant, Colo-rectal Cancer Section, Surgery Branch, National Cancer Institute. Physician Asst/Health Administrator, ACTION/Peace Corps. Lecturer, University of Washington School of Public Health & Community Medicine. Co-founder, Country Doctor Community Clinic. Seattle. Medical Detachment Sargeant & Clinical Specialist, U.S. Army, Istanbul, Turkey. Clinical Specialist, Intensive Care Post-Operative Ward, U.S. Army, Vietnam. AUTHOR: Clinical articles in Annal of Surgery, AJR, Surgery, the P.A. Journal, et al.

Walter M. Kearns, Treasurer

Medical Doctor, Surgeon,(Princeton Universit, B.A., 1944; John Hopkins University, M.D., 1947). Private Practice, Canoga Park, California. Clinical Professor of Surgery, UCLA School of Medicine. U.S. Public Health Service, 1952-54. OTHER: Member, Physicians for Social Responsibility. AUTHOR: American Surgeon; Wisconsin State Medical Journal; and other surgical literature: Treatment of Ulcers & Hernia.

Elizabeth Poe Kerby

Journalist.
Correspondent, Time, Life, and Fortune (Los Angeles). Staff, Time magazine. Information Specialist: U.S. Soil Conservation Service. Staff, Baltimore Evening Sun. AUTHOR: "The Conquistadors" (Putnam, 1969). Publications: L'Express (Paris); Christian Science Monitor; The Nation; Frontier; San Diego; Los Angeles Times; UCLA Monthly; Research Associate, "Report on Blacklisting: The Movies"; Fund for the Republic; et al.

Maryann Mahaffey

President, Detroit City Council.

Elected to Detroit City Council, 1973; reelected, 1977, 1981, 1985, 1989 (top vote getter in city). Professor, School of Social Work, Wayne State University, 1965-90. President (first woman), National Association of Social Workers, 1975-77. President, American Orthopsychiatric Association, 1984. Founder, Detroit Welfare Rights Organization, 1962. Volunteer Recreation Worker, Japanese-American Internment Camp, Camp Posten II, Arizona, 1945. Organized first integrated Girl Scout troop in Indianapolis, Indiana, 1952. OTHER: Recipient of Bill of Rights Award, Michigan ACLU; George Crocket, Jr. Award, 1990. Member, National Council of Negro Women. Lifetime Member, NAACP. AUTHOR: "Investigation of Social Services in Chile" in 1978 for International Federation of Social Workers. Co-Editor "Practical Politics and Social Work"; "Policy on Women", International Federation of Social Workers; Testimony on Social Work Policies, Congressional and State Legislative Committees.

Nancy G. McDermid

Dean, School of Humanities, San Francisco State University, CA.
Former Chair, Department of Speech Communication, San Francisco State University. Legal practice, Chicago. Teacher, Evanston Township High School & Community College. OTHER: President, Western Speech Communication Association, 1981-82. Board of Directors, ACLU of Northern California (Vice President; Executive, Equality, and Legal Committees). Liason to Academic Freedom Committee, National ACLU. Chair, Speech Education Committee, Western Speech Association. Chair, Freedom of Speech Committee, Speech Association of America. Chair, Academic Freedom Committee, United Professors of California. AUTHOR: Associate Editor, Quarterly Journal of Speech. Articles on Women's Rights; First Amendment; Social Policy; and Administration; et al.

Victor S. Navasky

Journalist.
Editor, The Nation, 1978-. Ferris Professor of Journalism, Princeton University, 1976-77. Visiting Scholar, Russell Sage Foundation, 1975-76. Guggenheim Fellow, 1974-75. Visiting Professor/Lecturer: Swarthmore College; Wesleyan University; New York University. New York Times, an editor. Founder, Monicle. Graduate, Yale Law School. OTHER: Member, National Council, Authors Guild of America; Member Executive Committee, PEN America. AUTHOR: "Kennedy Justice"(1971), Nominated for National Book Award. "Naming Names" (1980), a detailed study of the "victims" of the Hollywood blacklist, and of those who cooperated with Congressional Committees; Recipient, American Book Award; Articles of opinion for many journals in the United States and abroad; et al.

Gifford Phillips

Publisher.
Publisher, Frontier Magazine, 1949-68. Associate Publisher, The Nation 1968-1973. Trustee, Museum of Modern Art, New York City. Trustee, Phillips Collection, Washington, D.C. Member, Board of Governors, Yale Art Gallery. OTHER: Board, ACLU of Southern California, 12 years, 1950s-1960s. Chair, Legislative Committee, ACLU/SC. Delegate, Democratic National Conventions, 1952, 1956, 1960, and 1964. AUTHOR: Articles, The Nation; Art Magazines.

Ramona Ripston

Civil Liberties Executive
Executive Director, ACLU of Southern California & ACLU Foundation, 1987-. Vice-President Western Region, People for the American Way, 1986-87. Executive Director, ACLU/SC & ACLU Foundation, 1972-85. Board, National ACLU, 1986-87. Director of Public Information, National ACLU. Associate Director, New York and New Jersey Affiliates, ACLU. Co-Executive Director, National Emergency Civil Liberties Committee. Director, Public Affairs and Community Organizing, New York Urban Coalition. In 1960s, worked with SNCC and Mississippi Freedom Democratic Party. OTHER: Host, "Point/Counterpoint", KABC Talk Radio. Board of Visitors, Southwestern University School of Law. Member, Steering Committee of Statewide Pro-Choice Coalition. Adjunct Professor, University of Southern California. Member, Hollywood Women's Political Committee. Member, SHOW Coalition. Member, Board of Directors, Human Rights Watch. 1978 & 1988, Honore, People's College of Law, institution dedicated to recruiting and training people of color, feminists, and gay attorneys. Recipient, June Morrison Founders Award for 1980, for non-criminologist who makes outstanding contribution to justice in the criminal justice system. Recipient, Honorary Doctor of Law degree from the University of West Los Angeles School of Law. Honored as a Woman of Achievement by: Women For; Women in Communication; Southern Christian Leadership Conference; The Los Angeles City Council, and the Mayor of Los Angeles. AUTHOR: Has written extensively on: the First Amendment; Reproductive Freedom; the Voting Rights Act; Affirmative Action; the Rights of the Accused; the Death Penalty; U.S. Policy in Central America; and Poverty and Civil Liberties; et al.

Frank L. Rosen

President, District 11, United Electrical, Radio, and Machine Workers of America, UE, Chicago, Illinois.
International Representative, UE International Union, 1966-74. Union Shop Newspaper Editor; Shop Secretary; Chief Steward; Maintenance Electrician; Production Electrician; Lathe Operator; Goodman Manufacturing Company, Chicago. OTHER: General Vice-President & General Executive Board member, UE. Administrator, Local 1139, UE Group Pension Plan. National Co-Chair, U.S. Peace Council. National Vice-President, All Unions Committee to Shorten the Work Week. Board of Trustees, Anchor Health Maintenance Organization. Southwest Committee on Peaceful Equality. Chicago Committee to Defend the Bill of Rights. Circle Pines Cooperative. AUTHOR: Has written extensively on trade union affairs for trade union and related publications; et al.

Rabbi David Saperstein

Co-Director, Religious Action Center, Union of American Hebrew Congregations, Washington, D.C.
Rabbi, Congregation Rodeph Shalom, New York. Adjunct Professor, Comparative Jewish and American Law, Georgetown University Law Center. Former Chair, Washington Interreligious Staff Council and IMPACT. OTHER: Board Member: NAACP; Common Cause; Leadership Conference on Civil Rights. AUTHOR: Proclaim Liberty, Critical Issues Facing Reform Judaism. Editor of Resouce Manuals: The Challenge of the Religious Right; Preventing the Nuclear Holocaust; Social Action Manual.

For Your Information:

The National Committee Against Repressive Legislation (NCARL) can be addressed at the follwing locations:

National Office: 1313 West 8th Street, Suite 313, Los Angeles, California 90017. Phone: (213) 484-6661

Washington, D.C. Office: 236 Massachusetts Avenue NE, No. 406, Washington, D.C. 20002. Phone: (202) 543-7659

Midwest Region Office: 220 South State Streeet, Suite 1430, Chicago, Illinois 60604. Phone: (312) 939-0675

New England Region Office: 563 Massachusetts Avenue, Boston, Massachusetts 02118. Phone: (617) 236-4399

Northern California Office: P.O. 640354 San Francisco, California 94164. Phones: (415) 346-7350; (408) 624-7562

Northwest Region Office: 3933 Meridian N, Seattle, Washington 98103. Phone: (206) 634-1304

Southern Region Office: 1595 N.E. 175th Street, North Miami Beach, Florida 33162. Phone: (305) 949-6596

You Can Help!

Help the **First Amendment Foundation** Achieve the Widest Possible Distribution of this Educational Book.

Suggested Contribution (including postage and handling)

Single Copy $7.50

10 Copies $50.00

50 Copies $200.00

100 Copies $350.00

Make checks payable to **First Amendment Foundation**. Contributions are Tax Deductible.

Mail your Order to:

First Amendment Foundation
1313 West 8th Street - Suite 313
Los Angeles, California 90017